MW00831273

PRAISE FOR
THE RECONSTRUCTIONIST

"Jonathan J. Foster not only writes in creative ways, his insights into life and God consistently make me happy I'm reading his material. This book is no exception. I especially like the focus on love, which for Jonathan is what fuels the journey beyond deconstruction into the much-needed territory of reconstruction."

THOMAS JAY OORD
AUTHOR OF *OPEN AND RELATIONAL THEOLOGY* AND MANY OTHER BOOKS

"Jonathan J. Foster's *The Reconstructionist* is a wonderfully inspiring book on the subject of faith, doubt, deconstruction, and reconstructing well. For Christians who feel like they are walking on a waterbed rather than solid ground, Jonathan offers a deeply wise, pastoral, autobiographical, and hope-filled gem that will undoubtedly inspire others toward healing and integration. For those who are *dechurched*, *done*, *ex-vangelical*, and even faithfully Christian, this book will be a helpful companion for the journey!"

MARK KARRIS
AUTHOR OF THE BEST-SELLING BOOK, *RELIGIOUS REFUGEES*

"Life happens. And bad things happen to good people, all the time. Sometimes really bad things. Sometimes these things happen at the most inopportune times, like months into a new church plant, when you're giving everything you've got to do something great for God. That's not how it's supposed to work, right? Jonathan J. Foster's family tragedy carved out a well in him that was filled with grief and tears, finally transformed into a new experience of the love of God. It involved a costly, messy demolition and rebuild of the Christianity he thought he understood, resulting in a far more beautiful and resilient faith and practice. Jonathan learned that 'Love is change, and change is risk. Risk steps further into love and will peer into the cracks left by the earthquake until it falls into the cracks. Nothing is stable except for the destabilizing presence of love.' Jonathan learned that love can and does hold everything together. His book will make you think, cry, and then think some more."

PERI ZAHND

CO-PASTOR OF WORD OF LIFE CHURCH AND
AUTHOR OF *EVERY SCENE BY HEART*

"In *The Reconstructionist,* Jonathan Foster embraces brokenness and hope together and not in some cheap-ass sales-pitch kind of way. In the aftermath of unspeakable tragedy he finds, maybe for the first time, an authentic connection to God. A connection that has been stripped bare of the conventional constructs of theology, platitudes, posturing, and language. With little left to rely upon, Jonathan invites us along his journey into spaces that make unlikely and wonderful connections; like Aleksandr Solzhenitsyn and Kendrick Lamar. *The Reconstructionist* is a valuable resource for the spiritual refugee."

REV. RAJEEV RAMBOB

CO-HOST IRENICAST.COM / CO-PASTOR PARKSIDEUCC.ORG

"If you think church people and it's leaders are all neat and put together, then this book is gonna rock your world! I've known much of Jonathan's life journey, first as a member of his worship band in the late 90's, then as a friend and fellow seeker after that. Both of us, adult men looking for meaning and answers to life's challenges in the church, it's theology and beyond have always wanted more, and here Jonathan lays out the milestones of his faithful journey despite it's obstacles. Bold, daring and even pushing the limits of a neat and bow-tied 'Sunday morning best', which my generation was trained to present each week at the church doors, Jonathan has always been that one friend 'on the inside' who continues to pull the covers off the pretense of our narcissistic tendencies to push the walls of the church further open to all who may seek Him and his Grace. Big praise to Jonathan for sharing his experiences and its challenges for all to see and to gain wisdom from them. If you're ready for a reconstruction in your life, then this is the book to help you begin and maintain that journey."

DAVID ELLEFSON
INTERNATIONAL RECORDING ARTIST AND ENTREPRENEUR

"'Deconstruction' seems to be in vogue in some Christian circles—and not without good reason! It's easy to abandon one's faith in light of personal suffering or religious hypocrisy and intolerance. Jonathan has experienced both personal tragedy—the sudden death of his daughter—as well as a faith crisis which resulted in him leaving his denomination over a principled ethical stand. Yet through these challenges, Jonathan has emerged as a 'reconstructionist,' one who courageously re-envisions and rebuilds their Christian belief system as if refined by a purifying fire. What precisely needs deconstructing depends on where you begin and the religious baggage you carry. But the reconstruction process is broadly the same and begins at the cross. I am heartened that Jonathan is able to move forward holding fast to faith, hope, and the 'unruly rule of love.' This engaging book presents the scaffolding of his reconstruction and many on similar journeys will be encouraged to question and to persevere."

REV. DR. TIM REDDISH
AUTHOR OF *DOES GOD ALWAYS GET WHAT GOD WANTS?*
AND *THE JESUS I DIDN'T KNOW I DIDN'T KNOW*

"Whatever meaning-making system you use to make sense of your world, I invite you to grab your favorite drink and engage Jonathan as a spiritual conversational partner. I am convinced that this short book will help you to assess the life-limiting and life-giving aspects of your belief system. In a world where evangelicals are more 'up' on what they are against, Jonathan shows his hand as one who is more 'up' on what he is for. He is for mercy, people, and love. He does not propose a boundary belief system, but rather a set of affirmations that will surely invite you to re-evaluate the key anchor points of your faith. This short and very accessible work called *The Reconstructionist* will be well worth your time."

DR. JOHAN TREDOUX
AUTHOR OF *MILDRED BANGS WYNKOOP: HER LIFE AND THOUGHT*

THE
RECONSTRUCTIONIST

People > Text,
Mercy > Sacrifice,
and Love > Fear

JONATHAN J. FOSTER

Copyright © 2021 by Jonathan J. Foster.

First Edition

Cover design and layout by Rafael Polendo (polendo.net)
Cover illustration by theromb (shutterstock.com)

Unless otherwise identified, all Scripture quotations in this publication are taken from the Holy Bible, New International Version®, NIV®. Copyright ©1973, 1978, 1984, 2011 by Biblica, Inc.™ Used by permission of Zondervan. All rights reserved worldwide. www.zondervan.com The "NIV" and "New International Version" are trademarks registered in the United States Patent and Trademark Office by Biblica, Inc.™

ISBN 978-1-957007-03-8

This volume is printed on acid free paper and meets ANSI Z39.48 standards.

Printed in the United States of America

 QUOIR

Published by Quoir
Oak Glen, California

www.quoir.com

DEDICATION

For my kids
And their kids
(So on and so forth)

ACKNOWLEDGEMENTS

Yes, let's acknowledge a few people without whom this writing would not have seen the light of day: People in my various faith communities who have been with me through so much over the years. Old copyeditor-friends like Becca Thill and new copyeditor-friends like Julie Miller at editorialdeparment.com. Dr. Robert Duncan from NorthWind Seminary who asked me to put all of this on paper. All the young people in my life. Old ones too. You decide which you are. All coffee shops in Scottsdale and Kansas City. All musicians on that Apple playlist I had on endless loop while writing these words. All trails on all mountains everywhere. Dictionary. com. Every single one of the authors listed in the bibliography. The encouraging friends who subscribe to my Patreon page. And to Johnna, who had no idea she was signing up for any of this, but who keeps showing up day after day after day. I love you.

TABLE OF CONTENTS

THE INTRODUCTION PART 11
Where we talk about *Relief Art*, *You*, *Church Ex Nihilo*,
An Absurd Challenge, and *A Cracked Theology*

THE FIRST PART 45
Where we talk about *A Reconstruction Site Called People >
Text* and *The Corporeal World That God Is Interested In*

THE SECOND PART 61
Where we talk about *A Reconstruction Site Called
Mercy > Sacrifice*, a helpful *Thought Experiment*,
and thoughts about *René Girard*

THE THIRD PART 83
Where we talk about *A Reconstruction Site Called Love >
Fear*, how I *Triggered Their Scapegoating Mechanism*, *Hell*,
and the *One Word* this whole thing has to be about

THE DECOMPRESSION PART 113
Where we talk about *Systems of Goodness* and offer *The
Conclusion Where I Pretend to Bring It All Together*

THE BIBLIOGRAPHY PART 125

THE
INTRODUCTION
PART

RELIEF ART

Suddenly, in the middle of the monologue disguised as a
conversation over coffee, it occurred to me that the frustration
animating my friend's words was more about him than me.
I attempted to stay present, to engage, to listen. But it was
impossible. I was too distracted by the whirring of my mental
hard drive. Dozens of similar interactions were coming to mind.
Then a hundred. Then a thousand? I was unsure. The list just kept
growing.

I remembered a pointing finger there.

A red-faced word of condemnation there.

The yelling disapproval there.

I'm not necessarily troubled by conflict. I mean, given a choice,
I'd rather have someone agree with me than not, but no, it's
not the conflict that's troubling. What's troubling for me, what
crystalized in that particular moment, as I involuntarily compared
the anxiety of my friend's body language to the number of
files populating a little folder in the corner of my mind, is the

common denominator: all of them involve good, moral, religious, specifically Christian, *religious people.*

The theology and ecclesiology I wrestle with in this work, the humanity and beauty I'm attempting to name, is emerging against the backdrop of a lifelong collective conversation with the "religious person."

The more I listen and reflect upon the conversation, the more certain ideas take shape. I might, in a way, call this book a type of relief art. Relief derives its name from the Latin word *relevo.* It means "to raise." It's a centuries-old art form where artists create 3D images out of 2D backgrounds of the same material. While the background for my art, the religious context all of this comes out of, has certainly been altered, the point isn't to just alter. The point is to make art. In other words, it's not just deconstruction; it's reconstruction. I am a relief artist, *a reconstructionist.*

I don't mean to say that the 2D religious background has been all bad. There have been good times, great laughter, wonderful friends, helpful teaching, and support, specifically during tragedy that I do not forget. But I am concluding that we religious folk, in general, are not marked by love. We have been indelibly marked (mark of the beast?) by fear, rule-keeping, and sacrifice. And as I'll attempt to say throughout our time together, sometimes directly, sometimes indirectly, there just has to be a more beautiful version of Christianity. There *has* to be. Look around. The world needs a more beautiful Christianity. (And likely, more beautiful Muslim and Jewish faiths as well.)

We were supposed to be the ones known for our love.

We could still be. There's always hope. But it will take *reconstructionists* willing to forge new approaches to a very old subject: love. Love of God and love of neighbor. And, of course, the biblical test case for love of neighbor is love of enemy.[1] But in order to love your enemy, you must learn how to love yourself. Having been in the local church my entire life, I genuinely think most Christians don't possess love for themselves. I think they possess resentment, shame, anger, and fear. Or it possesses them. The fear has spilled over into a thousand errors, not least of which is a weird, entitled, pious kind of judgmentalism. It seems to be the drug of our choice. We Western Christians are basically religious junkies continually looking for whatever the next hit of judgmentalism can provide.

It's probably not that simple.

It probably is that simple.

Either way, we have wrecked ourselves.

---

1   A wording I've picked up on often in Wayne Northey's
    writing: www.waynenorthey.com.

What I'm attempting to do in this book is to pick through the wreckage and identify unhealthy ideologies; to reconstruct and find a more beautiful way. For what it's worth, I didn't set out years ago with any of this in mind. It was catalyzed in the middle of a particular and intense type of loss that served to knock the existential and theological wind out of me. I didn't see it coming. Blindsided, in the fullest sense of the word. I guess in one way, everything I write here is an attempt to grasp for air, to refill the lungs, to breathe again, to regain oxygen. I admit I write to you as a way to write to myself. And myself has been asking,

"What the *expletive* happened?

What's my *responsibility* here?

What does all of this *mean*?"

I imagine you already see the potential problem. Have you ever had the wind knocked out of you? Do you recall the pain and sense of desperation? Yes, when one loses breath, they'll do anything to breathe again. It's possible that in my pain and desperation, I am breathing contaminated air. It's possible as I identify an unhealthy ideology and point to new ways, I am infusing the new ways with an unhealthy ideology of its own. Do you see what I'm saying? The irony, given the way I started this introduction? The frustration animating my words here may say more about me than about you or anyone else.

THE YOU I'M WRITING TO

So it's true, I'm writing to myself. But I'm also thinking of, interested in, and therefore writing to you.

And I know you.

No really, I think I do. You're someone who has struggled with life, religion, loss, rules, heaven and hell, the church, injustice, fear, religious leaders, judgmental people, and every Facebook post that's touched on these subjects ever. You are on the verge of giving up on Christianity. Perhaps you already have. Politics, legalism, and hypocrisy are sickening to you. You're disillusioned, disenfranchised, disenchanted. And … I don't blame you for feeling or thinking any of these things. Actually, I applaud you.

I'll just tell you what I decided. I decided that if the religious people in my life continually reference …

- 1Thessalonians 5:22 to stay isolated *abstain from evil*

- Deuteronomy 7:3 to justify their reluctance at intermingling *not marrying otr ppls*

- Romans 10:9 to substitute a long obedience in the way, truth, and life of Jesus with a magic transactional prayer
Magic Prayer

bring a sword   *table flipping* → *goat separating*

- Matthew 10:34, or Matt 21:12, or Matt 25 to suggest Jesus was anything less than full of grace toward all people

  Jesus guilt offering
- Isaiah 53 to promote the idea that God needs sacrifice

- Hebrews 9:22 to convince themselves that <u>bloodshed can buy forgiveness</u>

- Romans 13:1 to suggest people are required to be subject to authorities while the authorities denigrate and disrespect a lower class of people and/or nation
  submit to authority

… then I should become an atheist. Because *those* interpretations and *that* god are doomed. I hope it's helpful for you to know that this was my decision. (And look at how well *I've* turned out.)

The frustration you are feeling is evidence you are open to something new. This is a good thing. None of us get to the new until we exhaust the old. And I don't mean to say everything about the old was bad. Thank God for the old. It was helpful and beneficial for a time. It worked. Until it didn't. But now? You're ready to become something more substantial.

I'm not trying to suggest that my ways are more substantial than the "old ways." Then again, maybe I am for why else would I go to all the trouble of writing this book? Either way, what I do think is that the contents of what you are reading is worth serious consideration. If you pull on its thread, it will lead you somewhere. That is the problem, though, isn't it? The "somewhere" that this all leads? *Sigh* … I feel my reluctance in encouraging you to read this, especially if you come from a more conservative Christian setting. Because if you pull on the thread with intellectual honesty, you will have to entertain questions. So proceed with caution. The deconstruction part of reconstruction is highly flammable. And I'm even not trying to sound edgy or cool when I caution in this way. (Wait, does any of this even sound edgy or cool? I don't even know what's cool anymore. As if I ever did.)

My hope is that some of the content will help you on your journey, although I readily admit, I am not the expert. Actually, I don't even think you need experts except for maybe one to tell you that you don't need experts. Everyone needs an expert like that in their life. But the real expert in your life is you.

I'm supportive of you.

I'm a fan of you.

I believe in *you*.

You, of course, have made mistakes in the past. It's okay. Forgive yourself, which I think means to give up hope that the past will ever look any different. You don't need to be perfect.[2] You can do this. You have the ability to think and come to your own conclusions. I don't mean to suggest that you can come to truth all by yourself. Given how interconnected we are, how intertwined our desires are, I doubt there's such a thing as "individual truth." So you won't find truth by yourself, *but neither will you find it without yourself.*

You have a lot to say, to give, to add, and to subtract. I have a feeling that far too many of us Christians give away too much of our authority, agency, and personal power to the preacher guy we listen to once a week on Sunday mornings.[3] (This is especially true for the people who have to listen to me.) I encourage you to vet what I'm saying. Read the resources I list in the bibliography. And then read the resources listed in *their* bibliographies. Listen. Watch. Reflect. Pray. Entertain questions. Search.

---

2   Mark Karris, *Religious Refugees: (De)Constructing Toward Spiritual and Emotional Healing* (Orange: Quoir, 2020), 21. "Self-compassion is key."

3   I say guy, because it's much more likely that your pastor (or priest) is male than female. If you're lucky enough to have a female pastor, I guess I would say the same things. I would still encourage you to not absolve yourself of vetting truth. Although as a rule I'm more inclined to trust females over males. Partly because love seems to have so much affinity *for* and *with* the powerless and between the two genders, there's no comparison as to who's been more powerless. Can we go too far with this logic? Probably. But maybe we should actually try it before we decide.

Most of all, listen to yourself.

If you come from an overly stringent Christian background, it's a strong possibility you've never received specific encouragement to listen to yourself.[4] That's not the kind of thing religious systems foster. They're much more interested in fostering the perception that listening to yourself is seeded in selfish rebellion and can only lead to disrespectful anarchy. But that's just not true. On the contrary, what's selfish and disrespectful is to shame people into thinking such things.[5]

I like what Mark Karris writes:

---

4   It's worth noting that my Catholic friends may have, in theory, a bit more freedom than us would-be reformers at assigning value to one's inner self. If the reformed folk are right, then humans are so messed up we could never dare trust ourselves. How could we when we've fallen so short of God's standards? The Catholic view, if I'm understanding correctly, provides a bit more space. It understands people to be marred, yes, but at least offers one the possibility of getting to truth even though one hasn't prayed the "sinner's prayer." I suspect the distinctions get blurred in the real world though. So it's probably a moot point. But, for what it's worth, in this I'm happily more Catholic than Protestant. As if either group is lobbying for my allegiance.

5   Howard Thurman, in his 1980 Spelman College commencement address, said, "There is something in every one of you that waits, listens for the sound of the genuine in yourself—and if you cannot hear it, you will never find whatever it is for which you are searching ..."

> You are not a bitter, prodigal son or daughter who chose to take all the beautiful things you learned, along with your rich inheritance of the Christian faith, only to squander it in some big debauched and satanic soirée. Instead, the well of your heart has been poisoned by various elements of current Christian principles, practices, policies, and attitudes at the hands of well-meaning churches.[6]

If you're new at "listening to yourself," just try it for a little while today. Then a little more tomorrow. Start small and work your way up. You can do this. Pause often to remind yourself of your agency. It doesn't mean you're disrespectful just because you question. You have the freedom to lay aside intimidating preachers, derisive father figures, shameful voices, limiting options, and wrathful gods. You can always pick them up later.

For now, breathe.
Protect your heart.
And listen to the sound of the genuine.

Finally, I think it's important to say, if you find you are not agreeing or not yet ready to agree with what I'm attempting to say, it's okay. I mean, read the whole book before you give it a one-star review. I know it's extremely rare for a Christian to make a rash judgmental decision, to say something disparaging before

---

6   Karris, *Religious Refugees*, 29.

getting the whole story. Still, in the off chance that you are in the practice of doing such things, my encouragement is to assume positive intent and read the whole thing.

Then again, do whatever you want. Who am I kidding? It's your life. Yes, *your* life. Run with it. Enjoy it. My only real encouragement is to find a God who runs and enjoys life with you. If you can't find that within Christianity, search elsewhere. It's an honor to be free, to search, to own your future.[7] So as we often say around my little faith community:

Choose your thoughts.

Be intentional about what you dream.

Pray with expectation.

Keep going.

God invents history in interaction with people who don't give up.

---

7   Solomon said, "It is the glory of God to conceal a matter; to search out a matter is the glory of kings." And Gregory of Nyssa said, "The reward of the search is to go on searching. The soul's desire is fulfilled by the very fact of its remaining unsatisfied, for really to see God is never to have had one's fill of desiring Him." And Bono said, "I still haven't found what I'm looking for."

CHURCH EX NIHILO

A few years ago, the idea of starting a new faith community sparked and jumped, convulsed and zapped along the vacuum of emptiness that was my life. Yes, it was all very metaphorical like that with ideas, frustrations, and innovations acting as little particles of energy bouncing around, interacting, and colliding. Just like creation. First, there was nothing—well, a quantum field of nothing as the physicist might say, or a "nothing-something" as Augustine might say, or "the face of the deep" as the writer of Genesis might say—and then there was something.

No monies, and then there were monies.

No denomination interested, and then there was a denomination interested.

No people, and then there were people.

No building and … wait … there's still no building.

The "big bang" of all this activity served to catalyze the movement of my little family east from Arizona to Kansas, from the known to the unknown ("not knowing whither they went").

The easiest "particle of energy" to understand, the most straightforward reason for the church's existence, might be that my previous employer no longer needed my services. I'm not saying one shouldn't have more profound motivations when starting something as significant as a church; I'm just saying I was jobless. And churchless. Which is how it works when you're a pastor. Your job is your church.

Trust me. I looked for openings. I asked around. I contacted some contacts. And connected some connections. (I even thought about leveraging some levers and liquidating some liquids, but I didn't want to get carried away.) I investigated, searched, and researched. I fasted, prayed, and reprayed. I knew I wanted something different, something I hadn't experienced yet.[8] Yes, I wanted to find an authentic place, a place where I could be myself. Years of seeker-sensitive, attraction-oriented, production-minded faith settings had left me hungry for realness, a place where one could entertain complex issues with humility and intellectual honesty. (Ha, *that* narrowed the options.)

I looked and looked, but … no dice. So I gambled and started something new.

Gambling, it occurs to me now, doesn't really go with humility and honesty. Oh, well. "You play the cards you've been dealt,"

---

8   If you have been connected with churches I've been connected with, I don't mean to suggest that *nothing* significant, authentic, or helpful occurred. I know good things happened. Rich relationships were formed. I have many fond memories. And even if I did suggest that, then given that I was the lead pastor in some of those settings, I bear primary responsibility.

as the saying goes. Moses got a burning bush and a cool staff. Rick Warren got a dream and a map. Me? I got ninety days before the severance ran out. Oh, and lest I'm downplaying the metaphysical, the spiritual, the "prompting of the Spirit" too much? Yes, I felt it was the right gamble to make.

Starting a new faith community from scratch will give even the most committed leader reason to pause. No money? No people? No building? Good grief, these are formidable problems. Even still, the intangibles are more formidable. I attacked the challenge like any seasoned veteran: I bought a black ballpoint pen. BIC, if you must know. And a small notebook. Moleskine, discreet, nothing too big. I mean, I didn't want the whole world to see what I was writing.

I created bullet-point lists.

- Vision: How would we talk about the unseen and the unknown enough to excite but not too much to overwhelm?

- Style: Compared to other churches within the denominational world (or other churches within the evangelical world), would we have a similar or different ethos?

- Distinctiveness: What would we offer right in the neighborhood that made us distinct from other worshipping communities?

- Identity: Would we be known for getting more people present on a Sunday morning, or for getting more of us present to our community the rest of the week?

- Leadership: Could we de-clergify the process, develop and celebrate others? Or would people expect the pastor to always take the lead?

- Theology: Would freedom be afforded us by the denomination or even by the people who might wind up attending each Sunday? Would we be able to approach pressing problems without the baggage of past expectations, tradition, or dogma?

AN ABSURD CHALLENGE

The bullet points went on and on: expectations, momentum, sustainability, staff development, community involvement, and more. Yes, to navigate all those things while pursuing humility and intellectual honesty would be very difficult. And I've yet to name what would prove to be the most significant challenge: navigating all the above in the middle of personal crisis, for on

January 1, 2015, eighteen months into the start of the church, our daughter was killed.

A wreck

lasting a few seconds

the damage

lasting forever.

The disaster sprung upon us without warning. No supernatural prompting. No insider information. It was an earthquake of an event, triggering a chain of blasts within the infrastructure of our lives. A cloud of grief, like so much debris after an explosion, hung in the air. Months and months. Years. In many ways still there, clouds shifting and morphing, a murmuration of heartache. Eventually, some of it began to settle, each existential thought a particle of dust swirling, floating, corkscrewing down through shafts of sunlight.

One thought that kept drifting around was the following:

If one can lose something this priceless, then one can lose anything.

More than once, I watched it float around my head, disappear, then reappear again in the airstream. I would reach my hand out. Palm up. An invitation for it to settle. To slow down.

God, just let it slow down. Let me hold it. Let me consider this thing. But no matter how deliberate my movement, it would tumble away. Into the breeze. Slow motion. So untethered from the gravity of reality that weighed me down.

Eventually, it would reemerge. Virtually the same thought, but slightly different: losing something this priceless points to the reality that ultimately, we lose everything.

So there you have it. Like Kafka, I've figured out the meaning of life is that it ends. And then, like Ellul, I've figured out the meaning of God is limited by the love that takes up residence beside us in our search for this meaning of life.[9]

A limited love.

Who would have guessed?

Our daughter was, as we say, one of a kind. She was full of personality, artfulness, life. Beautiful with all her little flaws. Perfect with all her slight imperfections. She was wild. And fun. And noisy. Her eyes the color of waves, marine and undomesticated; her personality too.

---

9   John Caputo, *The Weakness of God: A Theology of the Event* (Bloomington: Indiana University Press, 2006), 34. Caputo references Jacques Ellul from *Anarchy and Christianity* by saying, "Suppose that God's power over human beings is limited by love and that God takes up a place beside them in their powerlessness?"

Surely, she was the best of me.

Of my wife.

Of us.

Being her dad was the best. Not being her dad after only twenty brief years was (still is) the most absurd challenge.

It is remarkable and severe to lose something so priceless, but to do so while pastoring; to invite change within a group of people with so much changing within you; to be the interpreter of events with so much in your own life needing to be interpreted … well, there are no words to describe the difficulty. (Literally. I just spent a few minutes perusing my dictionary to confirm once again that there are no words.)

Should I have stepped down from any leadership role? Was I asking too much of myself to pastor while dealing with the loss? Should I have resigned, acquiesced, given up? Maybe. *Honestly?* I don't know.

Should I even be writing about it right now, six years removed? Am I asking too much of myself to write while dealing with the loss? Maybe. *Honestly?* I don't know.

I do know I'm trying to bear witness to this thing, but what does it mean to witness something? More specifically, what does it mean to witness something when one's entire framework of witnessing has been dismantled? How does *that* work? In the introduction of James Alison's *Faith Beyond Resentment*, Dr. Alison says, "To come across broken pieces and try and put them together is one thing. To discover oneself among the broken pieces which are being put together is quite another."[10]

There was no way to prepare for such absurdity. There were no real answers. I knew things would be different. I knew I had been affected. How should I put it? It was like something had moved, or shuddered, or groaned within me. It was deep, very deep. Delphic. Subterranean. The ink lines of my existential Richter scale had flown off the page in both directions. It cracked the construct of my theology. But there was no real way to assess the damage. It was life, in real time, with no point of reference. It was happening all around us, underneath us, within us. There was no way to know the right move, as if there was a "right move." We decided, for better or worse, to acknowledge the crack but to move forward.

---

10 James Alison, *Faith Beyond Resentment* (New York: The Crossroads Publishing Company, 2001), x.

A CRACKED THEOLOGY

To catalog all that was triggered by my cracked theology would go beyond the time we have together. We'll have to approach it, for our purposes here, less *khronos*-oriented and more *karios*-oriented. Less interested in timelines and more interested in fault lines. And as best I understand it, significant fault lines developed then cracked open in three theological locations.

- The first opening went right through my approach to the Bible, its purpose, and how I interpreted what it was I was reading.[11]

- The second developed underneath my conceptions of sacrifice and mercy.

- A third fissure ruined most—if not all—my thoughts about fear, punishment, and love.

The damage was totalizing. There was nothing left to do except to figure out ways to reconstruct. And after a few years, that's what I realized I was doing. Reconstructing. What does that look

---

11   And my interpretation of what was reading me. It's one thing to read Scripture. It's another thing to allow Scripture to read us. I've begun thinking that interacting with the sacred text is a bit like taking a Rorschach test. What we say about it says something about us.

like? Well, for me, it's walking, hiking, running, praying, breathing, reflecting, being alone, and being still.

And reading. Good grief, so much reading. A thousand pages, a few thousand more, a few hundred thousand more? It's never stopped. It's just generated so much thinking. I suppose reconstruction, for me, can be summed up in that one word: thinking. Ilea Delio says, "Thinking is a form of love."[12] I hope that's true. If so, I should be very loving.

Maybe you wouldn't categorize the events along your journey as traumatic. Or maybe you would.[13] Either way, it's led you to the place where you need to rebuild. And if I can do it, you can do it. You certainly have one advantage over me in that I didn't have what's contained in this book yet. I was working it out in real time.

---

12 Ilio Delio, *The Unbearable Wholeness of Being: God, Evolution, and the Power of Love* (Maryknoll: Orbis Books, 2013), 19.

13 I'm not sure it's helpful to categorize one's pain. Isn't it all relative? Does it really matter if someone else appears to have had worse pain? What does that even mean? Who decides that anyhow? If you've experienced something bad, then allow yourself to feel bad. There's a saying in the therapy world, "Your pain is your pain." (Actually, I think it's "Your shit is your shit," but I don't want to alarm any religious people who've made it this far in the reading. So we'll stick with pain.) One shouldn't overlook Brené Brown here. She says, "Stay in your own lane. Comparison kills creativity and joy." Brené Brown, *Rising Strong* (New York: Random House, 2015), 195.

I wasn't really thinking about being a reconstructionist. It's just what happened while I was unrolling giant spools of yellow caution tape in and around the mess above the various fault lines of my theology. I would pick through the wreckage. Separate the debris. Sit with, meditate upon, then run the length and depth of each fault line. I would descend into the rock and study the stratum. After time, I began to notice patterns in the rock. Certain sequences and arrangements. They started appearing, fading away, then reappearing. Little by little I gained the confidence to name the three construction sites.

People > Text.

Mercy > Sacrifice.

Love > Fear.

And now I'm ready to invite you on a tour. So get your hard hat on. And goggles. Roll up your pants. Wait, why do you need to roll up your pants? Leave your pants alone. Okay, are you ready? Walk with me. As we approach some of the new (or is it ancient?) theological architecture, I need to offer three general thoughts.

First, none of the building sites exist separate from any of the other building sites. They all overlap, dovetail, and flow together. To have clarity in one is to begin to have clarity in another. I can't imagine gaining understanding about mercy, for example, without reflecting fully on love. Similarly, I can't imagine an increasing awareness of love without increasing awareness of humanity's beauty. It's all interconnected.

So if you struggle in one area, the encouragement is to continue to the next. It's likely that in the overlap, you'll find clues to help you work both forward and backward. If you don't find clues, if you're not gaining traction, then it might be best to put it all aside. I have no desire to frustrate you or frustrate the way you construct meaning. The timing may not be right for you to read this. Or maybe you'll never want to read this. I don't know. Either way, it's your choice, and there will be plenty of exits along the way.

Second, if you choose to continue, please know that to duck underneath the caution tape and critically assess any of the fault lines is to invite a measure of destabilization into your life. This is particularly true for those of us who come from a more ordered, hierarchical, religious background. It's the religious people— my people—who have the most work ahead of them. It's the religious people who will feel the most uncertain, unsure, and untethered about all this reconstruction.

If you begin to feel untethered, rather *when* you begin to feel untethered, just know that this is normal. These are major shifts to consider, so it's natural to feel anxiety. Kierkegaard said,

"Anxiety is the dizziness of freedom."[14] Yes. Amen. It's freedom that allows us to interact with these issues. Freedom will set you free, but first, freedom can be overwhelming.

It will be in your best interest to do this work slowly. And with a licensed therapist. And maybe with a strong drink. Not necessarily in that order. None of the reflecting we're doing here will help you gain more certainty, power, or security. As you peer into the crevices, sooner or later, you'll fall into the crevices. I wish there were a different way, but I'm afraid that's just the way this works. That's the process, the unending pattern. Deconstruction is like a fractal image that never quite stops folding in on itself.

I can't really explain why this is the case, but to the degree that I can assign responsibility, I point to capital L-Love. Love is wounded and, as such, is on a never-ending inward journey full of uncontrollable risk (and uncontrollable promise). In philosophical language, this is where we might say that the *absolute* experiences *lack*. In theological language, this is where we might say that God experiences loss.

---

14 Soren Kierkegaard, *The Concept of Anxiety: A Simple Psychologically Oriented Deliberation in View of the Dogmatic Problem of Hereditary Sin.* (Princeton: Princeton University Press, 1981), 61.

Yes, loss. I no longer hold to the traditional view that God's perfection means he is unaffected by suffering. Namely, because God is love. Suffering is always involved with love. Then again, suffering is involved with a lack of love as well. It's not as if circumstances can be arranged in a way that one is able to avoid suffering. I'm trying to find that unstable middle ground in between the reality that love doesn't insulate us from pain and God not authoring the pain. If he authored pain, we would be forced to live by the myth of redemptive suffering which is not something I'm willing to do. (Also, if he authored pain, I wouldn't like him.) So, yes, suffering is involved with love. If love could control, there would be no reason for risk and there would be no way we could call it love, for love can't be love unless it can let the other walk away.[15]

Love is change. Change is risk. And risk steps further into love. It will peer into the cracks left by the earthquake until it falls *into* the cracks. Nothing is stable except for the destabilizing presence of love. The veneer of control is continually being peeled back by the chaos of chance and timing. By the way, it's being peeled away by the antagonism of evolution in biology, by the absurdity of super-positioning in quantum physics, by the incompleteness of the incompleteness theory in mathematics

---

15 To wrestle more with the concept of an uncontrolling
    love, read Thomas J. Oord. One good reason to do so is that
    he has a book titled *The Uncontrolling Love of God.*

too! Nothing is stable. Things fold in on themselves again and again. The dimensions can't hold the weight; it's a kaleidoscopic giving way to that which is ever on the inside. Everything good is fractal.

Third, as enjoyable as it is to speak in all this "fractal-philosophical" language, the goal, I think, is to figure how all this makes sense in the world. Yes, in real-life, flesh-and-blood ways. This is why Jesus is so central. He was the embodiment of all that is good and fractal. As such, he was the fulfillment of all that it means to be fully human.

 If humanity finds its first and divided archetype in Adam, it finds its second and undivided archetype in Jesus. The first was marked by faithlessness and scarcity, but the second was marked by trust and abundance. The first motivated by stinginess, the second motivated by grace. Adam blamed Eve, who blamed the serpent, a trait we see repeated by Cain, who blamed his brother Abel. But Jesus went in a different direction.

Rather than blaming, he chose to identify with those who are *blamed*.

Rather than offloading his anxieties onto a scapegoat, he chose to *become* the scapegoat.

Rather than validating the wheel of injustice fueled by our surrogate victims' blood, he *became* the victim. In doing so, he became a spoke inserted into the very wheel of injustice itself!

We see the spirit, will, or intentionality of Jesus to love in all of this. He was neither forced nor coerced to live the way he lived. No, he lived this way of his own volition.[16] He chose and followed love, or maybe the sequence is followed and *then* chose. Either way, it was love to the end. And at the end, on the cross, he experienced the loss, the risk, the mystery of love folding in on itself. Yes, everything good is fractal.

For how else could one begin to consider the one responsible for life handed over to death?

How else could one begin to reflect upon the maker of trees hanging on a tree?

How else could one begin to explain "the very God of very God" experiencing loss?[17]

How else could one begin to think of the Word being reduced to silence?

How else could one begin to talk of the Son of God crying out to Father God, "My God, my God, why have you forsaken me"?[18]

I speak this way not because I am unaware of atonement
theories but because I'm *all too aware* of atonement theories, particularly the *penal substitutionary atonement theory* lacing

---

16 John 10:18 (NIV).

17 A line from the Nicene Creed.

18 Matt 27:46 (NIV).

the fault lines of so much religion in the West. This is the theory that suggests God willed the death of his son to alleviate his wrath, something like a ransom paid, which winds up initiating a circular transaction. God pays God … to spare all of God's children … God's wrath. As David Bentley Hart says, this act of God would be "rather like a bank issuing itself credit to pay off a debt it owes itself, using a currency it has minted for the occasion and certified in its value wholly on the basis of the very credit it is issuing to itself."[19]

I categorically reject the idea that God needed the death of his son to forgive. And while I'm categorically rejecting things, something one doesn't get to do every day, I'll add that I do not believe God forsook his son for even one moment. I don't deny that Jesus cried out, but it doesn't necessarily follow that he was abandoned, any more than God abandons any of us when we cry out, which we all have surely done. No, God doesn't abandon his own.

S(He) is not willing that anyone should perish.

S(He) sticks closer than a brother.

S(He) is close to the brokenhearted.

19 David Bentley Hart, *That All Shall Be Saved: Heaven, Hell, and Universal Salvation* (New Haven: Yale, 2019), loc 353, Kindle.

How close? So close that s(he) goes into death with us, to redeem us, and in the process redeem death from the inside out, so that we can now say there is no God-forsaken place left in the cosmos. Is there any location love will not go? How could we separate ourselves from God's presence? Where could we go from his (her) Spirit? By the way, how could such a location exist? *What would that even mean?*

I'm not suggesting I or any of us can explain all that happened as Life collided with Death on a hill outside of Jerusalem some two thousand years ago. What I am suggesting is that I have been able to disassemble theories that painted me into a corner (yes, again, unstable construction) where I had no other recourse than to see the magnanimous, gracious, God of all creation as a petty, vindictive, child abuser.

That just doesn't make sense.

What *could* make sense is to say that in the cry of Jesus on the cross, we find evidence of what it means to be fully human. To be fully human is paradoxically found in the loss of God. That is the antagonism, absurdity, and incompleteness of love. For the cross was a risk brought about by love. Catherine Keller says, "The crucifixion is not what redeems, but what expresses the risk, the stakes, of radical love."[20]

At the cross, the Embodiment of Love dies, and love folds in on itself.

The dimensions cannot hold the weight.

The earth quakes.

The curtain tears.

The sky goes dark.

The seed dies and falls into the ground.

Pick your symbolic language, but I'm calling it a kaleidoscopic giving way to that which is ever on the inside. *Sigh* ... it's true ... everything good is fractal. And simultaneously, everything good is corporeal.

Augustine once beautifully blended the conceptual with the corporeal as he preached.

> *Man's Maker was made man,*
> *that He, Ruler of the stars, might nurse at His mother's breasts;*
> *that the Bread might be hungry, the Fountain thirst, the Light sleep,*
> *the Way be tired from the journey;*
> *that the Truth might be accused by false witnesses,*
> *the Judge of the living and the dead be judged by a mortal judge,*

---

20 Catherine Keller, email message to author, Dec 30, 2020.

Justice be sentenced by the unjust,
the Teacher be beaten with whips,
the Vine be crowned with thorns,
the Foundation be suspended on wood;
that Strength might be made weak,
that He who makes well might be wounded,
that Life might die.[21]

It makes no sense. And it makes all the sense. Like I said, a cracked theology.

---

21 St Augustine, *Sermon 191.*

THE
FIRST
PART

A RECONSTRUCTION SITE CALLED
PEOPLE > TEXT

Okay, we're at the first significant reconstruction site of our journey. Please keep your hands and feet in at all times. Actually, no, do the opposite. Get out and wander around as much as you would like. I think that's the point.

Let's talk about people and the Bible a bit.

Paging through the gospel story to find evidence of Jesus subordinating people to law, scriptures, or tradition is a fruitless endeavor. Not only did he refuse to place the law over people, but he often did the opposite. He lifted people. He esteemed them. Irrespective of their identity or origin. It could have been the foreigner, or the foreigner from a hated country, or the foreigner from a hated country who was a woman, or (big breath) the foreigner from a hated country who was a woman who had been divorced. (Gosh, what a quadruply bad person *she* was.) The point is, in every instance, as people left their interaction with Jesus, they seemed to leave feeling esteemed, elevated, and empowered.

Except for the Pharisees

Go ahead. Try it. Pick any person Jesus came in contact with and hold them in your mind's eye. Let their image emerge out of the story. Let their face materialize in front of you. Be present to them. Now, ask yourself, did Jesus care more about the person you are in the presence of ... or more about the law?

As I flip through the gospel stories and scan through the faces of thieves, hypocrites, prostitutes, extortionists, criminals, and outsiders, I can imagine only one case where someone might remotely suggest that Jesus seemed to care more about the tradition than the person. And that would be the somewhat enigmatic story of his interaction with the Syrophoenician woman in Mark Chapter 7. But, even if the interaction began with a sarcastic exchange (by the way, a fair way to interpret the interaction) that devalued the woman, by the end, Jesus was more than willing to change his mind and bless the woman. Considering all this leads me to some conclusions, then some questions:

There is a place for the written word, but is it above human beings?
There is a place for tradition, but is it above friendship?
There is a place for expectation, *but could it ever be above grace*?

I encourage you to consider what Jesus said about the Sabbath. When the religious leaders came to him upset that he had "worked" on the Sabbath, he responded, "The sabbath was made for humankind, and not humankind for the sabbath."[22] Consider expanding, superimposing, or infusing the truth of this thought throughout all of life. Consider being flexible with "the rules" in order to dispense grace with human beings who might be different from you.

If you try this, be forewarned, you will surely have your own religious leaders come to you, upset with your perspective, perturbed your thoughts are deviating from standard Biblical interpretation (and by standard, of course, they mean *their* standard Biblical interpretation.) When this happens, like Jesus, you can humbly respond, "The Bible was made for man, not man for the Bible."

And then things will get serious between you and the religious folk. And you know what that means: an invitation to get coffee together.

And over coffee, the well-behaved crowd will respond to your puzzling commitment to the importance of people by reminding you that Jesus came not to abolish but to *fulfill* the law. This is something you can agree with. It's true; Jesus did fulfill the law. You can nod, wait a moment, then say, "But does that mean he came to enforce all the rules, codes, regulations,

---

22 Mark 2:27 (NRSV).

and stipulations of the law? Or does it mean he came to fulfill the *intent* of the law?"

And when those good, probably well-intentioned, but over time thoroughly entrenched religious leaders furrow their eyebrows and clench their teeth in the manner of Clint Eastwood, well, you can attempt to alleviate the tension in the coffee shop by sliding around to their side of the booth to pat their shoulders a bit. You know, like you do when your dog is barking at the mailman outside the front door? I mean, you know the mailman on the porch is harmless, so you try to calm the dog with some gentle patting (*such a cute doggie*). Anyhow, when the religious folk squint their eyes, chomp down on their toothpicks, and ask you what you mean, you know, about your question regarding the intent of the law, you can slide over to their side, pat their shoulders, and say, "What I mean is the *intent* of the law. The *point* of all this." Look out into the expanse of the room, get them to follow your gaze, throw your arms open wide to indicate the options are endless, and say, "You know, my friend, where all this is *going*."

It's almost a guarantee they're not going to get it, which is why we're talking about it now, so you're going to want to have a backup plan, like a treat or something. Yes, give them a treat and then do your best to explain that the law's intent wasn't to be burdensome. The trajectory wasn't to take a few hundred regulations and turn them into a few thousand regulations.

The law's goal wasn't to create an objective list of rules, the execution of which would put humans in good standing with God. Behavior doesn't change God's view of us any more than behavior changes any healthy parent's view of their child. Playfully shoulder-bump your moralistic friend as you let them know they are in good standing with God. Yes, we are *all* in good standing with God.

Give the barista a high five.

Buy mochas for all the kids in strollers.

Good grief, God loves us!

Here's the good news: they're going to agree with you on the "God and love" part. That's the thing about the religious folk: they kind of think they have a corner on love. So trust me, they're going to be with you there, which is good. It's going to buy you a little time. Use it wisely. Because the bad news is, they've never critically worked through all the implications of what it could mean if God is actually love.[23]

So you are going to have to explain love isn't transactional. It's relational. The law's intention was to help humans treat

---

23 My favorite opening line to a nonfiction book comes from Mark A Knoll: "The scandal of the evangelical mind is that there is not much of an evangelical mind." Mark A. Knoll, *The Scandal of the Evangelical Mind* (Grand Rapids: Eerdmans Publishing, 1994), 1.

each other well. Spell it out if you have to, but the point is, humans can't treat each other well if they're subordinating, making second class, or otherwise looking down upon others for not "following the rules." Rules certainly serve a purpose, but they should always be administered with care, lest those who become the best rule-followers gain the power to shun, scapegoat, remove, or vote off the island those who are the worst rule-followers.

The sin of judgmentalism is something of a double bind that's built right into the fabric of any rule-following system. It's what makes it easy for us to see the hypocrisy of the Pharisees attempting to gain Jesus's endorsement in excluding the woman "caught" in the act of adultery while simultaneously blinding us to the hypocrisy of contemporary religious leaders trying to earn God's endorsement in excluding the gay person. Yes, like I said, a double bind. The double bind gets us to abuse some laws to fulfill other laws. It convinces us to huddle with the ninety-nine and call it good while Jesus is off with the one. No one even misses Jesus in most Christian churches because everyone is being so Biblical.

Ah, but I don't mean to mislead you. The people you'll be in conversation with probably have a perfect church-attendance record. These are the kind of people who will not take kindly to your suggestion that behavior is overrated. Eventually, they'll ask you that question, the one that crescendos both in volume and condemnation as each word is pronounced, the question that has done more to unify the well-behaving community than any creed, prayer, or commandment spoken, or act of love performed. Yes, everyone's favorite question:

"But what about *sin*?"

When they ask you that, you say, "Yes, yes, I'm all for talking about our sin as long as we make sure to talk about the sin of those who benefit from getting to define and then point out the sin."

Immediately following that response, take a long and satisfactory draw on your quad long shot grande in a venti cup half calf double cupped no sleeve salted caramel mocha latte with two pumps of vanilla and extra whip cream.[24] Make sure to wipe your mouth with the entirety of your forearm. You will have spoken truth.

---

24 Check out "Lunchbox Attempts To Order "The Longest Order Ever" At Starbucks." http://www.kick104.com/2018/07/11/lunchbox-attempts-to-order-the-longest-order-ever-at-starbucks/

THE CORPOREAL WORLD THAT GOD IS INTERESTED IN

To talk about sin outside of relationship is pointless. When we pursue love we *have* to be in relationship. We can't save what we don't love. And we can't love what we don't know. The life of Jesus compels us to get *to know others*.

At the risk of repeating myself, this isn't just an abstract love. This isn't just a "fractal-philosophical" love. This is a love rooted in the ground of relationship: God, humans, creatures, the world. "For God so loved *the world*" is how the well-known verse goes. It doesn't say, "For God so loved individual souls who are independent one from each other." No, it's the world. This world, our world, is the proving grounds for love. Jesus was a creature of the world. As Elisabeth Johnson puts it,

> Born of a woman and the Hebrew gene pool, Jesus of Nazareth was a creature of earth, a complex unit of minerals and fluids, an item in the carbon, oxygen, and nitrogen cycles, a moment in the biological evolution of this planet. Like all human beings, he carried within himself the signature of the supernovas and the geology and life history of the Earth. The atoms comprising his body once belonged to other creatures. The genetic structure

of his cells made him part of the whole community of life that descended from common ancestors in the ancient seas.[25]

He grew up in a very real world of Hebrew religion, family, and traditions within a wider context of Roman violence and hierarchy. It wasn't an experimental, hypothetical, virtual world. It was the real world.

His formative years would have been marked by thoughts of injustice, persecution, and despotism, living as he and his family did in occupied territory. It's very possible that he and his father, on the road between towns, looking for work, came across mass crucifixions like the one that happened in Sepphoris just a few miles from Nazareth around his preteen years. He would have struggled with that experience and others, juxtaposing them against Malachi's writings, Jeremiah or Isaiah, those prophets he so often quoted as an adult; the gap between who he knew God to be and how people lived would have been a great weight.

His mother spitting prophetic utterances about "God looking out for the lowly" and how Hebrew Lives Matter would have caught his attention and made an impression on him as well.

---

25 Elizabeth Johnson, *Deep Incarnation: Prepare to Be Astonished.* https://www. secularservites.org/wp-content/uploads/2019/04/Brzail-Johnson1.pdf.

Further formative would have been the agrarian culture with its harvest and seeds, its rain and drought. The air, the water, the sea, the hillsides.

All of these things would have and apparently did play a role in the development of his life. They all came together in authentic and vital ways in the world where he lived. They caused him to have a unique take on the point of the law. It was about helping us know others. Which is to say *love*.

Love in the world,

for the world,

for the people of the world.

With Jesus, the command is never, "Follow the rules." The command is, "Love your neighbor."

The lawyer, of course, asked Jesus the question, "Who is my neighbor?" It's essentially the same question we all ask. Who is our neighbor? Our enemy? The one lost sheep? The work associate? Yes, yes, yes, and yes. And according to Jesus, also the wildflowers and the sparrows as well. Our neighbor is the world, everything within the world, things that benefit us and things that seemingly don't benefit us: the bodies and creatures who receive our attention and the bodies and creatures who so often don't receive our attention.[26]

It's a love for God and love for people. Because how you love people is how you love God. And the point is, people come from and live in *the world*. It's surprising how far adrift we are from the Judeo-Christian claim that this whole thing started with a God who partners with the sacred ground (e.g., the world's soil) to create human beings. Ironically, in the light of its misunderstood history, Christianity is a worldly rather than otherworldly religion.[27]

The written text—the word—is inspired, but what it's inspired to do is lead us to Jesus. (The one who John refers to as The Word.) If you have a problem, take it up with Jesus. *He's* the one who said to the religious leaders of his day,

---

26 Johnson, *Deep Incarnation*, 3. "Repeating the question of the lawyer who challenged Jesus, Brian Patrick asks, 'Who is my neighbor?' His answer: 'The Samaritan? The outcast? The enemy? Yes, yes, of course. But it is also the whale, the bird, and the rain forest. Our neighbor is the entire community of life. We must love it all as our very self.'"

27 I borrowed the essence of this line from a thought-provoking essay by Mark I. Wallace titled "Green Mimesis: Girard, Nature, and the Promise of Christian Animism" from *Contagion: Journal of Violence, Mimesis, and Culture* 21 (2014) 1–14. Published by Michigan State University Press. https://works. swarthmore.edu/cgi/viewcontent.cgi?article=1224&context=fac-religion.

You have your heads in your Bibles constantly because you think you'll find eternal life there. But you miss the forest for the trees. These Scriptures are all about *me*! And here I am, standing right before you, and you aren't willing to receive from me the life you say you want.[28]

 Jesus never encouraged us to think of salvation as a prayer that's followed by rule-following behavior to gain safety in some postmortem, disembodied heaven. No, Jesus encouraged us to think of salvation as imitating his very corporeal behavior: to love others such that it could usher in the kingdom of God right here, right now.

Rules and prayers are only essential in that they help us to love. The rule of the text doesn't save us; we're saved by love. I'm not suggesting the written word isn't important. But Christianity is not the same thing as the Bible. Christianity is more like the forest that grows out of the soil of the Bible.[29] The forest of Christianity grows and moves in ways the written text cannot.

- The forest can cultivate a grove of anti-slavery trees even though the Biblical writers do little to condemn slavery.

---

28 John 5:39 (The Message).

29 I'm adapting this thought from something I heard Brian Zahnd talk about at his 2018 Water to Wine Conference.

- The forest can bloom a field of egalitarian flowers even though the Biblical writers are divided about the role of women.

- The forest can encourage an interconnected, peaceful ecosystem even though its Biblical writers are so often exclusionary and violent.

The movement, trajectory, and arc of the forest nourished by the River of Life and the Light of the Son provide life to all people, even people who don't measure up to the rules of the system— *especially those who don't measure up to the rules of the system.* This is grace that the soil of the written text cannot always give us. Or better yet, this is the grace the soil provides for those with the humility to see it. It takes effort. It's costly. It asks us to unclasp the hold we have on peculiar "literal" readings of certain passages. (Yes, quotation marks because to read the Bible *literally* is to understand that great portions of it were literally written not to be literal. How, for just one example, do you literally read poetry? You have to literally understand it as non-literal.)

The people who are unwilling to get their head out of the soil, as James Alison says, are in,

"the last gasp of a struggle, already several centuries old, desperately to try to get sense out of Scripture without letting go of power, and learning instead to read the texts from the only place from which they can fruitfully be read, which is in the company of the crucified and risen victim as he accompanies his disappointed disciples to Emmaus. Scripture as vulnerability to God rather than Scripture as protection from God!"[30]

Yes, Scripture as vulnerability rather than protection.

If you dare to be vulnerable rather than following certain invulnerable interpretations of the text, plan on one of your Biblicist friends shooting you a message over Facebook to say, "I just have too high a view of Scripture to agree with what you are saying." It's fifty-fifty on whether they'll attach a little angry-face emoji or a sweet little red-heart emoji. The beauty from their perspective, of course, is that either emoji works. They have a little and angry god who justifies their little angry emoji. But the heart also works because, again, they think they have a corner on love. Their whole system, laced and relaced with anger, fear, and sacrifice mixed up with love is almost foolproof. (Except surely I'm a fool, and *I* began to recognize the errors. So, there's hope!)

Emojis aside, do your best to patiently explain that it's not your view of Scripture that is being diminished. What's being diminished is your dogmatic hold on fearful, judgmental, and xenophobic *interpretations* of the Scripture.

Thank God, people are greater than the text.

---

30 Alison, James, *Faith Beyond Resentment*, 104.

THE
SECOND
PART

A RECONSTRUCTION SITE CALLED
MERCY > SACRIFICE

We're entering the second rebuilding site now. Keep your hard hats on and watch where you're stepping. I've been reevaluating all my preconceived and dangerous ideas about sacrifice. It's tricky, but I'm grateful to be rebuilding around something more substantial.

It's called mercy.

Mercy is what motivated Jesus to think of people as more important than the written law. It motivated the way he talked and the way he lived. He dispensed grace, with every person, at every opportunity. The religious people were scandalized by how freely he forgave. (As if he could just forgive. Silly Jesus.) They couldn't wrap their closed-off little minds around the way he squandered grace on those who feasted and drank, the lady who washed his feet, the man who was brought to him on a stretcher, or the blind man he met by the side of the road.

And the stories he told? If you really listen to the stories, it seems he believed nothing was needed to gain his Father's attention.

No offering.

No bloodshed.

No immolation.

When the son returned home in the Prodigal Son story, Jesus didn't portray the Father sputtering in anger. He didn't have the Father hesitate. He didn't have the Father say, "Wait, bring me a stable boy to whip and beat first. Then my anger will be satiated. *Then* I can forgive." No, he just forgave. (As if he could just forgive. Silly God.)

I listen to the story of the Prodigal Son and Jesus's other stories. I watch his actions and his ministry. I see his life and death. I take all of this together and arrive at a stunning conclusion: God doesn't need oblations, rituals, or surrogate victims. Nothing. You don't even have to accept God into your heart; the only thing you need to accept—to borrow from Paul Tillich—is that you're already accepted![31] How great is that?

---

31 Paul Tillich, *The Shaking of the Foundations* (New York: Scribners, 1948), 161–162. "Sometimes at that moment a wave of light breaks into our darkness, and it is as though a voice were saying: 'You are accepted. You are accepted, accepted by that which is greater than you, and the name of which you do not know. Do not ask for the name now; perhaps you

Mercy *is* greater than sacrifice.

Your moralist friends will be hesitant about such loose talk. The squinting, toothpick-biting, Clint Eastwood types will already have self-selected out of friendship with you, so we're probably talking about the next round of righteous folks at this point. They, too, will want to grab a coffee with you. (Good Lord, where in the world would American Christianity be without Starbucks?) If you try to talk about Paul Tillich with them, they're not going to be happy. They'll rub their foreheads, avoid eye contact, and eventually clear their throats to say something authoritative-sounding like, "Well, I believe in the full counsel of God's word." (Bless their religious hearts.)

Well, it turns out I believe in the full counsel of God's word too. So, let's think a little about how sacrifice plays out across the width and breadth of the Bible.

---

will find it later. Do not try to do anything now; perhaps later you will do much. Do not seek for anything; do not perform anything; do not intend anything. Simply accept the fact that you are accepted!' If that happens to us, we experience grace. After such an experience we may not be better than before, and we may not believe more than before. But everything is transformed. In that moment, grace conquers sin, and reconciliation bridges the gulf of estrangement. And nothing is demanded of this experience, no religious or moral or intellectual presupposition, nothing but acceptance."

THOUGHT EXPERIMENT

I invite you to sit down and engage in a little thought experiment. Imagine rounding up the cast of men who contributed to or were some of the main characters in the Bible. Go ahead, use your imagination and pull them all into a small auditorium. There are about forty of them or so. You've got your Jeremiahs and Isaiahs, your Ezras and Nehemiahs, your Pauls and Timothys. On and on. Yep, usher and wave them in. Let them know there are plenty of seats. "That's right, find your places, everybody. Yes, thank you. Hi, nice to see you. Yes, please leave the sheep outside. There you go. Okay, thank you."

You get all of them seated and quiet. I mean, it takes a while for some of them to stop talking.

Sheesh, Solomon? Constantly giving advice. And John the Revelator's got his little section all stirred up with some over-the-top scary stories. And then there's the writer of Hebrews—what was his name again? You scratch your head, but honestly, you don't know.

Anyhow, you get all of them seated and quiet, which is an act of God in and of itself. And then you walk across the front of the room, preparing to pose a question. At one side of the room, you spin on your heels and raise your chin for effect. You know you've always wanted to do this, so this is your chance. Spin the heels and raise the chin! You locate yourself in the middle of the presentation area. You scan the room, so excited to hear how the full range of Biblical writers will respond. You hold up an index finger and ask them one question. Just one question.

"Does God … require sacrifice?"

I ran this little thought experiment in my mind one time. And in *my* room, the question was followed by an awkward silence … and then … all *Gehenna* broke loose.

Holy cow, did the Levitical priesthood guys make a ruckus! They locked arms, rugby style, and began pulling in guys right and left. You should have seen some of the smaller prophets. They were all caught up in the scrum. It was a mess. I saw Malachi's head emerge, then get sucked back down. Then someone else, I think Obadiah? He wasn't having much fun. Then I saw someone's backside, unfortunately at the same time his robe got pulled over his head. (Thank the Lord it wasn't Noah.) After a minute, Amos shoved his way out, which created an opening for Hosea. Both those minor prophets, such cute little guys, shook the dust from their sandals and moved to the other side of the room.

The New Testament guys took calculated steps backward. Paul had his hands out to both sides, like a safety guard at a crosswalk, attempting to keep everyone behind his outstretched arms. Some of the guys didn't take kindly to Paul trying to take the lead, though everyone had to admit he had more reason to boast than anyone else. So yeah, as I saw it, the NT group formed their own backward moving mass.

And then there was David. He never stood. He watched everyone do their thing. Sitting there. By himself. Well, I guess after a minute Solomon came over. Yeah, he played with a toy chariot or something, just kind of drove it all around David's feet. You know, making chariot noises and stuff.

Well, the priests decided to answer the question first. (Surprise, surprise). They started in with their diagrams and dogma. Rules and regulations. They made a zealous plea, yeah, a real *Sheol* and brimstone presentation about the need for sacrifice. It was very convincing, especially with Moses standing in the middle nodding with that spooky staff of his.

David remained seated. Interesting. He seemed conflicted by what the Levites were saying. When they finished, he scrunched up one side of his face and shook his head, saying, "Uh, I don't know. I mean, maybe." He didn't sound very convinced. He continued, "I tried it both ways, but I gotta say, I just don't think God is super happy with burnt offerings." He shook his head quietly for a second, you know, really giving it some thought. He opened his mouth as everyone leaned forward and held their breath. Then he closed his mouth, which triggered a collective exhale. He opened his mouth again … but waited. Everyone inhaled. This process repeated a few times. Enough, in fact, that Zerubbabel (a lot of the guys called him Big Z) started breathing into a paper bag. David's opinion was obviously no small thing. Finally, he broke the silence, "Yeah, no, God doesn't delight in sacrifice."

Big Z collapsed into a chair. Moses and the Torah guys threw their hands up in the air. A few of them made fists and punched their open palms. There were boos and hisses. Funny, it didn't really seem to bother David. He was pretty chill. He just sat there. And then he pulled out an acoustic guitar. I have no idea where that came from, but he started writing a tune right there on the spot. It was amazing. Yeah, David was very cool.

Hosea and Amos stepped to the front of their little group and gave a nice presentation. Though I think a part of the reason it went so well was David's background music. Because honestly, their graphics sucked. But after David started playing? Things settled down a bit, like everyone had pulled an anxiety blanket over their shoulders. Hosea and Amos concluded with a few pie charts that made absolutely no sense but then paused, looked at each other, and without equivocation said, "Look, God's into mercy, not sacrifice."

It's weird how the debate never really came to a conclusion. Paul talked about the importance of being free from the law, including sacrifice, but there were other times he admitted he'd done his best to live in obedience to the law like he'd done in Jerusalem right before he was arrested. He certainly indicated that God meant for Jesus to be a final "sacrifice of atonement by his blood," but that opened up a real can of worms about how to approach atonement.

Abraham was one of the few guys willing to stand up to Paul and frankly, he wanted to know how any of them could trust a God who demanded the death of his own son. Isaac stood right behind Abe, eyes as big as saucers, waiting for Paul to respond. It was an awkward moment. Paul shook his head and said a few other things, but no one knew his exact point. Sure, several of them pretended, but I'm not sure anyone *really* knew.

Then Matthew started speaking. Didn't even ask Paul's permission. Just stepped to the front of the New Testament gang and began talking about Jesus, which really seemed to galvanize the room. He told the story of how the Pharisees were once giving Jesus a hard time. Most of the men rolled their eyes and scoffed when he mentioned the Pharisees. Matthew had to wait a minute for the room to calm down. He continued, making a point to mention that what the Pharisees were upset about, in his words, "was how Jesus would hang out with all different kinds of people,"—Matthew started to choke up a bit as he continued—"including, well,"—he looked around the room— "people like me." He had a tear in his eye.

Moses raised an eyebrow.

Paul dropped his hands.

Solomon stopped making noises with his toy chariot.

Then Matthew said, "Jesus waved all the religious leaders over." Matthew emulated Jesus's movements by waving his hands to the group. All the Biblical writers shuffled forward.

shuffle-shuffle-shuffle

Matthew continued, "Yeah, he waved all the guys over until they were *real* close." He waved some more as he drew out the word *real*.

shuffle-shuffle-shuffle

The group was packed tight around Matthew at this point. Hanging on his every word. It was so crowded that some of the minor prophets (Nahum and Joel maybe?), like little hobbits, were climbing up the back of the group, crawling all over and on top of Isaiah's head.

Matthew waited a moment, then continued. "Then Jesus said, 'You know what I would like you guys to do?'" Matthew paused for effect. He peered into the eyes of the group even as he thought about standing next to Jesus, peering into the eyes of the Pharisees.

He said, "What I want you guys to do is to go and think about this thought …" He closed his eyes, raised his voice a bit, and repeated the word *go*, held it there for a moment, and then, pointing at Hosea, nodded and repeated what Jesus said. "Go and learn what this means … I desire mercy, not sacrifice."

It was so quiet. You could have heard a red-dyed goat hair drop.

Philemon stood with some of the minor prophets, fist raised in solidarity. Peter, James, and John all took a knee. Joshua stared into his sword, gazing intently at his reflection. Isaiah nodded wordlessly. Job wiped an eye. Some of the Leviticus guys hung back, smoothing wrinkled robes and chewing jagged fingernails. Moses looked back at them. Then at Matthew. He repeated the process. He started to say something but then decided to stay quiet, opting instead to tap his staff three times. Then he rested his chin on top of his hands, which covered the top of his staff. All he said was, "*hmm, hmm, hmm.*"

I watched all of this play out in my mind. I waited. Sat still. Waited a bit longer. But the Biblical writers never reached agreement. Matthew quoted Jesus, and then the room faded as if someone turned the master volume down. It's crazy, but there just wasn't unity among the Biblical writers on the topic of sacrifice. They were in disagreement with themselves. I finally realized that was just the way it was going to be. A certain number of them were saying, "Yes, God needs sacrifice." Another group was saying, "No, he doesn't." And others remained quiet. But in the end? They all deferred to Jesus.

I thought about all of this as the image in my mind dissipated. I decided I would defer to Jesus too. Mercy would be my goal.

I wonder who you will defer to?

It is true, of course, that sacrificial language is in the text. Even, at times, associated with Jesus. The writer of Hebrews says things like, "Christ offered for all time a single sacrifice for sins."[32] And Paul says things like, "God presented Christ as a sacrifice of atonement."[33]

So, if God is into mercy, what's going on with this talk of sacrifice?

If you're lucky enough to have any religious friends left, they are going to want to meet up for even more coffee and ask that question and more. They will really want to straighten out your thinking regarding sacrifice. I say go for it, but make sure to take your little pocket Bible with you. Wait? You do have a pocket Bible, right? You've got to get yourself one of those. Super handy.

---

32 Hebrews 10:12 (NIV).

33 Romans 3:25 (NIV).

Make sure, right up front, to impress upon them the idea that sacrifice doesn't need to be a blood payment on God's behalf. They've been told, in so many words, that it does, but it doesn't. For example, Jesus didn't go to the cross to appease God in the same way the Mayans sacrificed people to appease their God. God doesn't need death to forgive. God can simply (though forgiveness isn't always simple) forgive.

Furthermore, Jesus never once told someone they were forgiven, only to walk away and throw up his hands as he remembered to say, "Oh yeah, almost forgot. You are going to need to wait a few months to be really forgiven. Cuz that stuff I just said there? Yeah, it doesn't mean that much until I'm brutally tortured and murdered. But when *that* happens, you can count on it, then you will be forgiven."

Do your best to communicate these things, but rule-keeping people and sacrifice do not part easily. Sooner or later, they're going to get Biblical on you and quote one of their favorite verses: "There is no forgiveness without the shedding of blood." And when they do, this is where you whip out that pocket Bible, turn to Hebrews, and read the part they left out. Because the entire verse goes like this: "In fact, the law requires that nearly everything be cleansed with blood, and without the shedding of blood, there is no forgiveness."[34]

Then ask your friend, "Do we still live under the law?"

Before they answer, flip the page to chapter 10 and read verse 1: "The law is only a shadow of the good things that are coming—not the realities themselves." And then while you're on a roll—and if you haven't been on one, you will be now—read verses 4–7:

It is impossible for the blood of bulls and goats to take away sins. Therefore, when Christ came into the world, he said: "Sacrifice and offering you did not desire, but a body you prepared for me; with burnt offerings and sin offerings you were not pleased. Then I said, 'Here I am—it is written about me in the scroll—I have come to do your will, my God.'"[35]

Maybe your moralistic friend will finally realize sacrifice and bloodshed are more about the law than they are about love. Perhaps they'll see the error of their ways. It's even possible your friend will repent. Yes, right there in between sips of their overly priced caffeinated beverage. However, if they don't repent, try to get a butter croissant out of the deal. I personally go into

---

34 Hebrews 9:22 (NIV).

35 Hebrews 10:4–7 (NIV).

most conversations with religious people assuming that a butter croissant will be as good as it gets; but you never know, miracles can happen.

Pastry or no pastry, the sacrifice of Jesus doesn't need to be equated with a type of bloodshed to appease God. However, *there was bloodshed and appeasing needed.* It just that *we* were the needy ones, not God.

Propitiation is the big fancy theological word here.[36] Someone angry or offended needs to be handled with care, pacified—you know, *propitiated.* The red-faced driver yelling as he passes dangerously close on the highway? Yeah, he needs propitiating. The guy who comes home and kicks the dog after a tough day? Or the mom who leaves the snarky comment on social media? Or the preacher foaming and spitting at the pulpit? They (and we all) just need a little propitiating.

The point is, when we humans are offended, we expect others to pay a price. And if it's true for us, then we think it must be true for God. Because for many of us, God is simply a projection of who we are. If we need a pound of flesh, then he'll need a hundred pounds of flesh. If we get angry and vindictive when feeling slighted, then he must get super angry and vindictive. If we need

---

36 1 John 2:2 (NKJV). "He Himself is the propitiation for our sins."

propitiating, then surely, *he* needs propitiating. We make him out to be the biggest, angriest, most offended red-faced driver in all the cosmos.

We assume he needs sacrifice.
But he doesn't.
We do.

How could we begin to unpack this critical point? Well, this is an excellent time to take a break on our tour, sit down, take a drink of water—yes, reconstructionists need to stay hydrated—and talk about René Girard's Mimetic Theory.

RENÉ GIRARD

It was 2015. I was, to stay aligned with my earthquake metaphor, deep within the apertures of my cracked theology, attempting to wrestle with the mystery of death. I spent days, weeks, months spelunking. Deep down in the sedimentary rock, I found ancient cracks, breaches, and lines. I followed them up and down, back and forth. I kept discovering the same thing: all the questions I had about our girl's death were in some way or another connected to questions I had about the death of Jesus.

In other words, when I asked *Why would a loved one die at a young age?* I was also asking *Why did Jesus have to die at a young age?* When I asked *Where was God when our child died?* I was also asking *Where was God when Jesus died?* The creases and folds running through the stratum kept indicating that my best thinking about the one was intertwined with my best thinking about the other.

While making these connections, I came across the work of French anthropologist and literary critic René Girard. It was no small thing for me to discover his insights on ritual, sacrifice, and violence. We don't have time to cover all the angles, but allow me to highlight some of the more critical elements of Girard's Mimetic Theory.

A) Mimesis has to do with imitation. We are, in short, imitative creatures. Because we are influenced so much by others' desires, none of us knows what our own desires are, exactly. And so, we imitate.

Suzy wants what Maria has.

Maria wants what Diego has.

Diego wants what Bob has. (And Bob? He has no idea what he wants. Poor Bob.)

Multiply this about eight billion times, or whatever the current number of people living on the planet is, and what you get are a lot of people who are unsure about their motivations. What they want is what others want. And so, we spend our time imitating the other, allowing the other, as the psychoanalysts say, "to mediate our desire."

B) This is fine, as far as it goes, but problems arise when we perceive the objects of what the other desires—and now what *we* desire—to be limited. Scarcity, or the appearance of scarcity, engenders anxiety.

Thinking about Christmas gifts provides some good examples. Think Cabbage Patch dolls, or Beanie Babies, or Nintendo handhelds. Or think of toilet paper and hand sanitizer (to be clear, not good Christmas gifts) during 2020's early stages of the COVID-19 pandemic. The common denominator in these examples is how influenced we are by what others around us are doing to the degree that we see others as competitors and rivals. We buy then they buy. They buy more and we buy even more. Scarcity leads to rivalry. Once we enter into the rivalry stage, we inflame each other's desires. We act as models for one another. The cycle continues until conflict erupts. Associates, friends, and family are quickly drawn into conflict as well. And what began as a personal battle can escalate into something that threatens the peace of an entire community.

C) This is where it gets interesting. What Girard uncovered was the way communities (e.g., nations, tribes, companies, and dare

I say religious institutions?) standing at the precipice saved themselves from falling into violent disorder. It's humanity's ingenious solution to conflict: scapegoating.

Imagine a group of people fighting. Chaos and conflict growing. When the entire community is at risk of imploding, picture someone turning and pointing their finger at a solitary figure. It doesn't really matter if the singled-out person is guilty of anything or not. What matters is what I might call the transfer of energy. The victim now becomes a conduit that enables violence to travel from the group to the scapegoat. Blaming saves the community. As the tension offloads onto the scapegoat, it paves the way for punishment of the scapegoat. Even more, it *justifies* punishment of the scapegoat. It's a move built upon at least two lies, one about the victim's guilt and the other about the community's innocence.

Whether it's the Aztec throwing the virgin into the volcano,

Or the Nazi shoving the Hebrew into the gas chamber,

Or the American plantation owner lynching the African.

Or a thirty-three-year-old Hebrew man being hung on a cross.

Girard's mimetic theory allows us to see our systems are flawed. We thought the victim was guilty. We thought he (or she) was being punished for their sins. But it was our sin that led us to believe we could manufacture peace at the expense of a victim.

As Caiaphas says, "Don't you realize it's better for one man to die than for the whole nation to perish?"[37] Ultimately, what humanity has done well is to produce peace through violence.

Mimetic theory gave me a different lens through which to view the death of Jesus. And I began to get answers to the two questions I posed earlier.

Why did Jesus have to die? Answer: because we killed him. Where was Father God when His Son died? Answer: with him. He didn't turn his back.

The death of Jesus wasn't something God required. It was something that *revealed* God's heart. God fell into the cracks. Love risked and folded in on itself. Love didn't demand violence. Love absorbed the violence. The dimensions couldn't hold the weight; it was a kaleidoscopic giving way to that which is ever on the inside.

Everything good is fractal.

As for the interpretation of what happened at the crucifixion, I'm not going with the blood-thirsty, angry deity in need of

---

37 John 11:50 (NIV).

propitiation kind of a god. I'm going with the loving father who's willing to experience death with us kind of a God.

Mercy really is greater than sacrifice.

THE
THIRD
PART

A RECONSTRUCTION SITE CALLED
LOVE > FEAR

We are now touring the third reconstruction site. Nonsacrificial, nonviolent love is the most critical building material here. All my rebuilding has centered around the structural integrity of love.

Religious systems don't do well with love. There's just too much at stake, too many centuries of pinning down the truth, of getting everything straight and ordered. They've captured the truth, imprisoned it within their own understandings, but what exactly do they have behind bars?

It reminds me of the nineteenth-century Russian novelist (and no book is complete without referencing a nineteenth-century Russian novelist) Ivan Turgenev, who reportedly said,

> The people who bind themselves to systems are those who are unable to encompass the whole truth and try to catch it by the tail; a system is like the tail of truth, but truth is like a lizard, it leaves its tail in your fingers and runs away knowing full well that it will grow a new one in a twinkling.

If you choose to subordinate everything in your life to nonsacrificial, nonviolent love, you'll have a run in with the "lizard tail holders" sooner or later. They'll call you _weak_ and _compromised_ and use other highly technical terms like _wishy-washy_ to describe your values.

I admit love doesn't seem strong. It's so flexible. It seems vulnerable, porous. But like intertwined steel cables that support a massive suspension bridge, it's the flexibility that provides the strength.

The religious person has yet to discover this strength. They've built on the concretized foundation of dogma and tradition for too long. In my experience, the more you talk about love, the more they talk about fear. It's amazing. Fear is their god. And if you give them a chance to defend their god, look out. They'll gladly sacralize their response, marshal the troops, elect some Joshuas to send in, and wipe out every man, woman, and child that dares to defy their beliefs.

They'll sing battle hymns of the republic

until the cows come home to justify their beliefs,

their beliefs that undergird their fear,

their fear which is their god,

their god worth far less than the cows for whom they wait.

I can be harsh on the religious people because they're my people. I'm culpable in all of this fearmongering too. Fear is a way to rule. And though I'd like to say that I didn't use it to rule, that's probably not true. I have been known to participate in a system built upon scapegoating and surrogate victimization. It put me in a position of power. Okay, I wasn't trying to gain a position of authority, *per se,* but what exactly is going on with preachers, teachers, and religious leaders? Especially we North American, Caucasian, heterosexual male types? We've often been put in positions of power to reinforce the rule of the church, which only justifies our positions of power. (Yes, outstanding circular logic there.)

Sigh, I have to confess complicity. But thank God, I learned again that there are no more rules … *except for the unruly rule of love.*

The unruly rule of love is continuously moving, shaping, shifting. It's a self-donating, perpetually kenotic, fractal-like energy. It has no interest in power and at the same time has all the power. It became my strength in the months and years following our daughter's death.

I was so thankful to learn that God wasn't interested in hierarchical power that placed Him (Her) at the top of the organizational flow chart. If there is such a thing as a flow chart, S(He) is at the bottom, or better yet, infused within the flow itself. God wasn't separate from Christ at the crucifixion. He was "in Christ reconciling the world to Himself."[38] And in the Father's embrace of the wreckage on top of the hill outside Jerusalem, I saw the Father's embrace of the wreckage on highway 75 outside Wichita.

God was present to Jesus in his death,

who was present to our daughter in her death,

who is present to us in all our deaths.

The more I thought about it, the more I realized you could only say one of two things about a God so close to death: he was there either because he was directly responsible or because he was in solidarity with us. If it's the former, well, I have no need for a god responsible for death. We have enough of those gods. They're everywhere, not least of which in our religious systems. But if it's the latter, I'm thrilled because I do have need for a God of love, life, and solidarity.

---

38 2 Cor 5:19 (NIV).

TRIGGERING THEIR
SCAPEGOATING MECHANISM

Once I decided Jesus died because of humanity's scapegoating obsession, I looked around and noted who our current scapegoating victims are. (No shortage there!) Is there anyone being slotted into the scapegoating role more than LGTBQ+ human beings. Again, I didn't set out to make any changes. I just followed love. And it was clear that love was asking me to ask the denomination I had been a part of my entire life to stop the way they were scapegoating human beings who identified as something different than heterosexual. You can guess the outcome, and I go into detail about it in other places, but yes, I triggered the trap. It was inevitable that I would be scapegoated for pointing out their scapegoating ways. I find it all rather poetic. Who knew poetry could hurt so much?[39]

I saw the fear in their eyes, heard the anxiety in their voices, and felt the shame in their pointing fingers. Yes, at times, literally pointing fingers. And if I didn't know it by their body language, I knew it by their conversation because all they seemed able to talk about were things like sin, punishment, God's "obvious"

---

[39] It was only after they scapegoated me for pointing out their scapegoating ways that the real work began. For it was then that I had to decide not to scapegoat *them* for scapegoating me for pointing out their scapegoating ways!

design, fear, and their favorite topic: hell. You can imagine how much fun *that* was. The thought occurs to me now that it was a little bit like hell to hear them talk so much about hell. In the middle of all the hell they stirred up, they fortified their positions, staked their claims, and drew their lines.

One day, as I reflected upon all the different fearful energies feeding off each other, I thought of that insightful theological tome, *If You Give a Mouse a Cookie*. I became inspired from On High to write the following:

> If you give the tradition an excuse to fear, they're gonna circle the wagons. If they circle the wagons, it'll be a defensive move. Fueled by anxiety. They'll probably lose feeling in their extremities. And get tunnel vision. And lack courage to innovate. They'll decline in influence. The energy that could have gone into something good will be funneled into labeling an enemy.

> If you attempt to be gracious to their enemy, you'll find yourself on the outside. This will make it easier for them to differentiate from your ideas. This will make it easier for them to differentiate from *you*. They'll find scapegoating useful in building unity. The more you attempt to point out their scapegoating practices, the more they won't be able to see them. They'll ask you to get in line. Then label you misguided. Maybe sinful. And then *you'll* be the enemy.

> They'll feel free and clear to disassociate from you. They'll call this practice holy. They'll even gain a temporary uptick in growth

because of their holiness. They and their adherents will celebrate revival. Then they can forget about you. And dehumanize you. And you'll go to Sheol, Hades, the realm of the dead. Where nonpeople like you always go.

And there, Jesus will find you. Because Jesus will go anywhere to find the marginalized. You'll be astounded by grace, but the traditional system will likely miss it. They'll be busy. Holding conferences. Discussing religious things. It will afford them the seduction of control. Meanwhile, seductions will be controlling them. Every once in a while, they'll feel a squeeze. And a growing anxiety. They'll look themselves in the mirror. And if they look, *really* look … chances are the tradition will have an excuse to fear.[40]

It was strange to have followed love to the point of being scapegoated, but that's precisely what happened during Holy Week of 2019. I'm not sure how I feel about being shown the exit, but that it happened during Holy Week? The week we celebrate Jesus, being shown the exit by the powers? The anniversary of when it happened to Jesus? Well, that's interesting. (Yes, again, poetic.)

I harbor no ill will toward my former denomination. Partly because none of it was really about me; far be it from me to

40 *If you Give the Tradition a Cookie…* https://www.jonathanfosteronline.com/blog/2019/4/18/if-you-give-the-tradition-a-cookie

act offended at being scapegoated when LGTBQ+ friends and others have been experiencing it with much deeper intensity for centuries!

And partly because I recognize that in some ways, they had no choice; they, led by their angry gods, *had* to expel me. It was the only way they could keep from falling into chaotic disorder themselves. They simply reenacted humanity's age-old drama of scapegoating one person (and in this case, one church) to save their whole community. Yes, a reiteration and validation of Caiaphas's argument a couple of thousand years later. The scapegoat mechanism remains hidden for my old religious system, for they see, in the death of Jesus, a *reflection* of sacrificial patterns rather than an *exposing* of sacrificial patterns.[41]

In retrospect, I say,

> Thanks be to God, who always leads us triumphantly as captives
> in Christ and through us spreads everywhere the fragrance of

---

41 René Girard, *Battling to the End (Studies in Violence, Mimesis & Culture)* (Lansing: Michigan State University Press), 50. "The incredible news, the event whose import the Western world has not yet realized, though its own history has been increasingly determined by it, is that God is now on the side of the scapegoat victim. He is outside of the system regulated by the play of sacred difference, the difference that modern thought has brought back with unbelievable naïveté and violence because of fear of a common identity. This totality can end only in death and nothingness."

the knowledge of Him. For we are to God the sweet aroma of Christ among those who are being saved and those who are perishing. To the one, we are an odor of death and demise; to the other, a fragrance that brings life.[42]

And I say,

> The Christ faith enables us to inhabit the space of being victimized not so as to grab an identity but, in losing an identity, to become signs of forgiveness, such that one day those who didn't realize what they were doing may see what they were doing and experience the breaking of heart that will lead to reconciliation.[43]

Oh, and I also say,

> A church that cannot change in order to exist for the humanity of man in changed circumstances becomes ossified and dies. It becomes an insignificant sect on the margin of a society undergoing rapid social change.[44]

I name their actions as selfish, closed-minded, and even evil. It is remarkable how pragmatic the church can be when it comes

---

42 2 Cor 2:15–17 (NIV).

43 Alison, *Faith Beyond Resentment*, 172.

44 Jurgen Moltmann, *The Crucified God* (Minneapolis: Fortress Press, 2015), loc 336, Kindle.

to evil. And how evil itself becomes self-transcendent. Jesus posed a question once: "Can Satan cast out Satan?"[45] Apparently, the answer is yes. The Satanic can stir up hell, and then it can scapegoat, which proves to be cathartic for the community and something like a limiter for even more evil. Amazingly, evil is capable of containing itself, which helps it avoid destruction. Consider the Cold War, for example. During this uncertain time, nuclear bombs protected us from nuclear bombs. The very existence of nuclear weapons, paradoxically, prevented the world from disappearing in a nuclear explosion. Yes, evil can contain evil.

Was my excommunication as dramatic as the Cold War? Probably not, but I see the parallels. In my excommunication, I do not doubt that evil found a "healthy" outlet that prevented the denomination from a type of implosion. It wasn't a human sacrifice, but in a sense, it was. At the very least, it was an instinctual move that provided evidence of what Girard revealed: when all else fails, communities rooted in pagan notions of sacrifice will pursue peace through violence.

They, of course, don't name it as violence. Depending on the tradition, they'll call it Biblical, holy, or righteous. And yes, to be clear, there is a way to read the Bible that encourages people

---

45 Matthew 12:26 (NIV).

to call scapegoating Biblical, holy, or righteous. It's just not a reading inspired by love. It's a reading inspired by fear.

And once unity behind that reading is gained, it's almost impossible to notice the fear.

The more I reflected upon all of this, the more I realized how prevalent fear was in my religion over the years and, to be fair, how prevalent it was inside my own heart over the years. I repented of the fear and set my heart upon love. John wrote,

> God is love. Whoever lives in love lives in God, and God in them. This is how love is made complete among us so that we will have confidence on the day of judgment: In this world we are like Jesus. There is no fear in love. But perfect love drives out fear, because fear has to do with punishment. The one who fears is not made perfect in love.[46]

Why did John contrast fear and punishment with love in this passage? Maybe he had some of the same conversations that I've had and that you will surely have if you pursue love. Perfect fear can drive out love, but thankfully, perfect love drives out fear. I guess the question is, which will we focus on: fear or love?

---

[46] 1 John 4:16–18 (NIV).

HELL

Inspired by fear, the "gospel" in the West says that the sacrifice of Jesus was our ticket out of the most fear-inducing place: hell.[47] In one sense, I agree. The way of Jesus is our way out of hell, but not necessarily hell as some postmortem place of torture. What kind of God does that to his children, anyhow? I can't imagine torturing my child for one second, let alone all eternity. Instead, I think of hell as that metaphorical place of living under the weight of scarcity, of assuming there isn't enough grace to go around, of constantly offloading our sins onto the backs of others, which justifies our willingness to scapegoat. It's not abundant. Or gracious. Or merciful. Or human-being centered. (It's a hell of a place.)

We could repent, which means to change our mind. *Change our mind about what?* About our violence-inspired ways. That is, we could stop fortifying our positions and drawing lines. That is, we could stop with all the incessant fear talk and just accept that God is a gracious God who has already accepted us. But we usually don't.

---

47 I put *gospel* in quotations because the word *gospel* is supposed to mean "good news." But the penal substitutionary atonement theory at the root of the overwhelming majority of Christianity in the West is not good news. It's very old news about a very old and ineffective sacrificial system.

It's too costly.

Hell is a topic that goes beyond our allotted time.[48] But, let me at least point out that a massive problem we have in talking about hell revolves around language translation and context interpretation. One, at the very least, could be aware that our English Bibles have used the word *hell* in places and ways that may not be the most helpful to the modern-day reader. Three words play a prominent role throughout the Bible:

- *Sheol*, a somewhat nonspecific term referring to the shadowy, dark place where the dead go after life.

- *Hades*, a Greek word arising out of Greek mythology that seems to be a bit more "animated" than *Sheol*, but still, there's no consensus as to what it is exactly.

- *Gehenna*, the only one of the three words associated with burning, as it was a name for the garbage dump outside of Jerusalem. It had the terrible distinction of

---

48 I thought about spending more time on the subject matter here because it fuels so much of the religious person's actions, but honestly, writing about hell isn't that much fun and believe it or not I'm trying to have fun as I write. So for an extended look at what the Bible says about hell and what we could choose to believe if we wanted to, please do not miss David Bentley Hart's *That All Shall be Saved*, or Sharon L. Baker's *Razing Hell*—oh and while you're at it, definitely read Brad Jersak's *Her Gates Will Never be Shut*.

being the geographical location where some of Judah's kings sacrificed their children by fire.

A line that gets repeated a lot in moralistic circles is that Jesus talks more about hell than any other person in the Bible. And it's true. Kind of. Of course, no one else in the Bible talks specifically about it much, so it's not hard to be the person who talks about it more than anyone else. Even with that said, it's almost an irrelevant point because when he does talk about it, most often, he is referencing *Gehenna*.[49] *Gehenna* does not equate to our modern idea of hell. As we noted, *Gehenna* was the place where sacrifices took place in order to gain God's favor. (In other words, a place of penal substitutionary atonement!)

It is a reasonably intelligent conclusion to draw that Jesus is not referring in scripture to a postmortem place of torture. Rather, he's talking about a hell that can occur right here in this life, in the world. There's a passage in Luke, for example, where Jesus refers to a calamity that had occurred in a nearby community and follows it up with the line, "Unless you repent, you will all be destroyed in the same way."[50]

---

49 Luke 9:43, Luke 12:5, Matt 5:22–30, Matt 10:28, Matt
    18:9, Matt 23:15, Matt 23:33, Mark 9:43–47 (NIV).

50 Luke 13:1–5 (NIV).

Here's Brian Zahnd's commentary:

> For a host of reasons many people have been trained to read references to an afterlife hell into this passage. They assume Jesus is saying something like, "Yes, some people were killed by Pilate and others were killed in a building collapse, but I tell you, unless you repent, you're all going to hell when you die." But that's not what Jesus says at all. Jesus is not talking about hell, or at least not an afterlife hell. Jesus isn't talking about what happens to people when they die. Jesus is talking about an avoidable threat in *this* life. In effect, Jesus is saying, "Unless you rethink everything, embrace the way of peace that I am teaching, and abandon your hell-bent flight toward violent revolution, you're all going to die by Roman swords and collapsing buildings." This is exactly what happened forty years later when the city collapsed under the bombardment of Roman catapult balls (hundred-pound hailstones) and more than half a million people were killed by Roman swords. Jerusalem had become hell — a horridly real and literal hell![51]

So Gehenna, the concept Jesus most often refers to, doesn't equate with our modern-day version of hell, but neither does *Sheol* or *Hades*. None of them matches the image conjured up in the modern person's conscious when they hear the word *hell*. Our idea of hell has been hijacked by Milton's and Dante's

---

51 Brian Zahnd, *Sinners in the Hands of a Loving God* (New York: Waterbrook, 2017), 189.

writings, our own thoughts of retributive punishment, and years of Hollywood-inspired revenge. In short, we have little imagination outside of violence. We have little understanding of how discipline can be consequential without being something God inflicts upon people who misbehave.

God's not interested in severing relationships.

God is in the business of reconciliation.

God's not into wounding.

God is into healing.

Finally, I think it should be pointed out that most religious people in the West seem oblivious to the fact that neither the Biblical writers nor the early church fathers made dogmatic claims about hell. The Apostles' Creed simply states that Jesus was "crucified, died, and was buried. He descended to the dead. On the third day, he rose again." The Nicene Creed says even less about what happened after the death of Jesus.

But here's what I imagine happened. (And how else can we speak of such things without using imagination?) When Jesus died, he dropped like a seed into that space we might call afterlife. There, Death and all his friends gathered. They sneered, laughed, and groveled over the Son of God. But then something began to take place. The seed broke open and began to grow. It was just a shoot at first, but green enough to cause Death's minions to jump back. Green is not the color of afterlife. Then the green shoot turned into a sprout, a sapling, and then a tree. We might call it the Tree of Life.

The demons fled. Much to the shock of all afterlife's inhabitants, the tree grew until it filled the entirety of that space, breaking out into the entire cosmos as well. The tree influenced *everything*. Life changed Death from the inside out.

We can now say, "Death has been swallowed up in victory."

And, "Where, O Death, is your victory? Where, O Death, is your sting?"[52]

In all this, we have victory over our archrival, our nemesis, the thing that's been plaguing us throughout history: our fear of death. The writer of Hebrews makes this clear:

> Since the children have flesh and blood, he too shared in their humanity so that by his death he might break the power of him who holds the power of death – that is, the devil – and free those who all their lives were held in slavery by their fear of death.[53]

_____

52 1 Cor. 15:54 (NIV).

53 Hebrews 2:14 (NIV).

So, what do I think about hell? I'm not sure, but whatever it is, I believe it's been redeemed from the inside out. Jesus went into a type of *Gehenna*, the valley where we sacrifice children to earn God's favor, and broke the curse. There is no more God-forsaken place left in the cosmos![54]

I speak of these things because of how often the topic of hell has come up with my good and well-behaved Christian friends. It came up so often that in what turned out to be on one of the last Sundays of my denominational life, I stood in front of our faith community and said the following:

"Many of us have friends, family, and church associates in our lives telling us that by virtue of our commitment to love everyone, even the LGTBQ+ crowd, we are on the path to hell." I had a very captive audience at this point.

I looked around the room and continued, "I want to say to those folks that, first of all, we're sorry this has been so painful for you. We genuinely do not need for you to suffer. We wish this were easier for you." There were a few hesitant nods, but the majority of the group was with me.

"Secondly, we want to say that while none of this was our first choice, that it's okay. If we're headed to hell, well, then that's where we are going. Those of you who have written us off, you

---

54 Check out singer/songwriter Andy Gullahorn and his song, "God-Forsaken Place."

go on ahead to heaven, and we'll meet up with you later." A few smiles broke out.

"It's okay because Jesus has been to hell before us. And if Jesus has been there, it means there is no God-forsaken place left in the cosmos." More nodding and a few audible amens.

"We would have drawn this up differently if we could have, but there's nothing we can do about it now. We cannot unsee what we've seen." I channeled my inner MLK Jr. as a hand raised in the corner somewhere.

"We cannot unhear what we have heard," I said. Someone stood up in the middle.

"We have seen the light and heard the news. The news that Jesus is Lord of the living and the dead. The black and the white. The rich and the poor. And …"—pausing for effect—"the straight and the gay." A chorus of amens.

"So, for the folks who disagree with us, go on ahead in peace. We're going to go to hell. With Jesus. And we'll all meet up later. And what a day of rejoicing *that* will be!" An auditorium of applause.

It was a surreal moment in my life. I was in the middle of a scandal. And I had been led there by God![55] *Who knew?*

I was sad but strangely honored to be in that position. I decided in *that* moment, and am still convinced in *this* moment, that love is the most powerful agent in the universe. I have no desire to go back.

IF YOU HAD ONE WORD

If you had one word to describe the hope of the world, what would it be? If there were one explanation for why the wings of the Spirit bothered to hover over the mysterious waters of the deep, if there were one concept to summarize the beauty and complexity of the incarnation, if there were one word big enough to contain the hope of the kingdom of heaven, what would that word be?

Wouldn't it be *love*?

---

55 Alison, *Faith Beyond Resentment*, 179. "The scandal of the Gospel is not the heaviness of religious demand made on weak individuals, but the fact that the collapse of what seemed sacred is a collapse produced by God himself."

Not kitschy-valentines-card, or cheesy-romantic-comedy, or thinly-produced-four-minute-pop-song-love. Not love as that thing we've packaged, consumed, commodified, and otherwise cheapened. And to be clear, count me chief among those who've cheapened love.

No, not that kind of love; rather, love as in the dark matter, ubiquitous throughout the furthest reaches of the universe, swirling, fusing, holding everything together. As in the waterfall thundering from the highest peaks to the lowest canyons in pathos and humility. As in the elderly man stooping over at glacial speed to kiss his bride of sixty years as she lies in the hospice bed. As in the newborn in the crook of her momma's neck, resting, nursed, fully content. As in those who are willing to rethink everything for the sake of others. As in vulnerability with no assurance of safety. As in the refusal to scapegoat one more person.

Love, as in one who gives up power to identify with the powerless.

Yes, to whatever it is we've begun to identify in all the above. Then again, maybe we should quit while we're ahead (if one could say we're ahead). Perhaps we should stop trying to identify. Perhaps the more we attempt to identify and define, the more elusive love becomes. Maybe love knows of our obsession for taxonomy. And certitude. And certainty. Ah, maybe no one word can get at what we're trying to express. Or perhaps every word gets at it? Who can say, but I asked the question, so I'm sticking with it. What if there were only one word? What would the word be?

It has to be, *it must be* love.

Love is the singularity out of which all that is originates. Our origin is love. Period. Nothing else. Our origin is not sin. We don't have to be original-sin people. We could be original-love people. If we are original-sin people, that forces us to start with the problem and reduce the Son of God, the embodiment of love, to a fix of the problem. But humanity isn't a problem to be fixed; it's a mess of motives, dreams, hopes, failures, brokenness, and glory to be celebrated and loved.

Original-love people refuse to box people into binary categories of good and bad. Original-love people know atheists who are loving and Christians who are evil. It doesn't make sense, but it's the truth.

As Nobel Prize-winning artist Aleksandr Solzhenitsyn said, "If only it were all so simple. If only there were evil people somewhere insidiously committing evil deeds, and it were necessary only to separate them from the rest of us and destroy them. But the line dividing good and evil cuts through the heart of every human being."[56]

And as Pulitzer Prize-winning artist Kendrick Lamar said, "I got power, poison, pain, and joy inside my DNA."[57]

Humanity is complicated. But love can smooth out the jagged edges of complexity. Better yet, love lives at the very edges of complexity, piercing us, breaking our hearts, but in doing so, releasing hope deep within us. Love is our hope. Love is everyone's hope.

Our hope isn't in another list of sins for all of us to avoid, although I'm all for doing your best to avoid sin. The problem is, we can't even agree on which sins to include on the list. But imagine for a second that we could agree. It *still* wouldn't matter because we can't keep the list up to date. We humans are very good at sinning. The moment all of us good Christian people settled on an exhaustive list, sure enough, someone would figure out an entirely new way to sin!

---

56 Alexander Solzhenitsyn, Harry Willetts, trans., *The Gulag Archipelago, 1918-1956, An Experiment in Literary Investigation: Volume I* (New York: Harper & Row Publishers, 1978), 168.

57 "DNA" from Kendrick Lamar's album, *Damn* (2017).

After a while, you figure out that there has to be a better way to help people be better humans. And there is. It's called love. And love has something to say about how effective we've become at creating lists of sin and telling certain "sinful" people that they must change their behavior in order to abide by one of our lists. So bring on all the complications and complexity. Love can handle it all.

To follow love, we have to listen. Which isn't easy. The culture is loud. And the church culture might even be louder, driven as it can be by its delusion, ego, and vain repetition of potentially misleading dogma. Why, for example, do we gather by the millions to worship Jesus, to put him on a pedestal, to rally around his perfection? Is it so we won't have to think about how love's perfection wants to work itself out in us? Is it to absolve us of the responsibility of following love ourselves? Meanwhile, the Messiah never told people to bow down and worship him. He said, "Follow me."[58] The cross, regrettably, has become an object of magic, symbolizing *what* Jesus did rather than *the way*.

Yes, the church culture is loud and powerful. Meanwhile, love is so shy, continually inviting, never quite arriving. It's like a melody

---

58 Boersma, Hans; Daniels, T. Scott; Finger, Thomas N.; Weaver, J. Denny. *Atonement and Violence* (Abingdon Press. Kindle Edition), 128. Scott Daniels says, "It's one thing to thank and praise Christ for taking up his cross, it is another thing altogether for the disciple to take up his or her cross and follow him."

we've never heard before, yet familiar. But if we slow down, we may hear it whispering to the church something like, "*psst* ... slow down ... listen."

Yes, slow down.

Listen.

Climb out.

Get free.

Stop working so well.

Enough assembly-line evangelism.

Enough winning.

And power, and politics, and mega.

Enough of that design.

Maybe we could break that design.

It turns out it's already broken. The cornerstone of Jesus became the stumbling block to "that design." But we didn't pay attention. We paved over it with penal substitution atonement theories. We recreated systemic religious power structures and continued building on the faulty design of scapegoating and victimization. Yet there's no ambiguity about the real design of the church.

The *real* design, the *watermark* of the church, is the cross. It's not words, or manuals, or statements, or writing—that's right, throw this writing away—it's not books, or declarations, or websites, or mantras, or rules. There are no more rules, except one: *the unruly rule of love*.

Love is greater than fear. Not greater as in removing all chance, risk, and randomness. No, greater as in voluntarily walking with us no matter where we walk or what we walk through.

Solutions are great, but what we really desire is solidarity.

Answers are helpful, but what we really need is a friend who sticks closer than a brother.

Clarity comes in handy, but what we are really looking for is long-term communion.

This is what love offers: communion.

Jurgen Moltmann says,

> God does not become a religion, so that man participates in him by corresponding religious thoughts and feelings. God does not become a law, so that man participates in him through obedience to a law. God does not become an ideal, so that man achieves community with him through constant striving. He humbles himself and takes upon himself the eternal death of

the godless and the godforsaken, so that all the godless and the godforsaken can experience communion with him.[59]

He is God with us, the exact representation of God, the fullness of God, and the embodiment of the kenotic emptiness of God.[60] Follow Him. Not your rules.

When friends with the perfect tithing records get mad about the talk of love subverting rules, just remind them to read the text. This is *Jesus's* idea. He's the one who claimed to be the way, truth, and life.[61] He's the one who claimed the scriptures were about him.[62] He's the one who reinterpreted everything in the scriptures *in light of himself*. We could do the same if we wanted.

Many have told me that I pick and choose the scriptures I want to focus on. And my response is, "Yes, I do. Thank you for noticing." I think we *all* do. I'm merely attempting to be honest about it. And the scripture I choose as the most important? 1 John 4:16. I happen to think it's the pinnacle of the entire Biblical movement. It simply says, "God is love." Yes, and amen.

---

59 Moltmann, *The Crucified God*, 414

60 Matthew 1:21, Hebrews 1:3, Colossians 1:19, Philippians 2:6–8 (NIV).

61 John 14:6 (NIV).

62 John 5:39 (NIV).

Love is what I choose to build upon and build with. It's ecological, flexible, recyclable, organic, and forever self-sustaining.

You can't run out of it unless you stop giving it away.

You can't lose it unless you try and hide it.

You can't use it up unless you keep it for yourself.

There are three reconstruction sites in my life: Mercy, People, and Love. But the greatest of these is love.

THE
DECOMPRESSION
PART

We are now approaching the end of the reconstructionist tour. You can hand in your hard hats and take off your goggles. There you go, yes, thank you, brush yourself off. We're going to gather in a little makeshift room for a few minutes. I imagine this room as something of a decompression chamber, a place to reorient ourselves. Some of us have gone down deep. The air pressurization is different up top, so we'll want to pace ourselves and slow our reentry to not make ourselves sick.

Get some water, yes reconstructionists need to stay hydrated, and get plenty of rest. When I was young and people asked for input or advice about life issues, I'd usually open with a question like, "Have you read your Bible lately?" You know, something super spiritual like that. Now I'm more likely to ask, "Tell me about how much rest you are getting." Frankly, most of us just need a good nap.

SYSTEMS OF GOODNESS

I offer a few pages here as a kind of dialogue with my friend, Dr. James Alison, who himself is in dialogue with culture, church, and Biblical writers in a unique way. If you skipped this chapter and just bought his books it would be a better use of your time. However, since you're here in the decompression chamber with nowhere to go, you might as well finish this thing. (And then go and order his books.)

Before Alison, a word from the Apostle Paul:

> "Christ redeemed us from the curse of the law by becoming a curse for us—for it is written, 'Cursed is he who hangs on a tree …"[63]

Paul attaches the word *curse* to the word *law*. This is remarkable given how much emphasis the religious institution placed on the law. What purpose did the law serve? I think we can say that the purpose of the law was to set up markers, borders, and boundary lines in order to help determine right and wrong behavior. As such, it is easily interchangeable with such modern words and concepts as *tradition, dogma, statements, manuals, written confessions, creeds, rules,* and so on.

Paul seems to be telling us that when he voluntarily stepped into the place the law designated as cursed, even there, outside the system's lines of rightness, a place of new life was found. And most followers of the Christian tradition in the West numbly nod,

---

63 Gal 3:13 (NIV).

parroting what they've been taught, saying, "Yes, this is true. God set it up this way. God needed Jesus to be cursed to lift the curse for all of us." So on and so forth. And yet, now that you've taken the reconstructionist tour, you recognize the inaccuracy: God didn't need Jesus to be cursed. *Why did we ever think it desirable to have a god who needs curses?*

Alison says,

> No, for Paul, it was not God who had set it up for Jesus to be cursed at all. The sphere of the curse is what it looks like to live in a world in which good and evil are defined over against each other ...[64]

Again, the system (e.g., *tradition*, *dogma*, *statements*, *manuals*, *written confessions*, *creeds*, *rules*, etc.) is the vehicle by which we understand good and evil. In other words, we define bad by defining good. Then we separate the two with a boundary line. This explains our obsession with the law. Because if we stay on the right side of the line, we can call ourselves "good." But of course, it's only in comparison with those who are on the other side of the line. Which then explains our obsession with labeling others "bad"!

---

64 James Alison, *Undergoing God: Dispatches from the Scene of a Break-In* (New York: Continuum, 2006), 204.

Back to Paul, who in this case is quoting Deuteronomy:

> For all who rely on the works of the law are under a curse, as it is written: "Cursed is everyone who does not continue to do everything written in the Book of the Law."[65]

And just when we thought Paul was on the religious person's side, we realize he's turning everything upside down. Alison continues,

> For Paul is quoting the text not, as we would usually imagine it, as a proof text, a way of saying "you see, the text agrees with me." It doesn't agree with him. Rather he is quoting it as internal evidence of an anthropological structure. He quotes the verse so as to show that because it curses those who don't obey the Law the text of the Law itself shows that it is a part of a system of goodness which divides between good and bad, and thus that even those who uphold it, who are apparently blessed by it, *are in fact dwelling in the sphere of a curse.*[66]

If the law curses someone, it can only do so by playing by the system's rules. The system requires us to have bad people. It's only by having people to exclude that the religious can label themselves as good.

---

65 Gal 3:10 (NIV).

66 Alison, *Undergoing God,* 200, emphasis mine.

If you want a comedic if not accurate portrayal into how the logic of good systems breaks down, spend some time with the TV series, *The Good Place*. By the final season, Tahani, a status-obsessed character in the show, recognizes the ugly truth that's being revealed about humanity's preoccupation with exclusivity. She says, "The problem is, if all you care about is the velvet rope, you will always be unhappy, no matter which side you're on."[67]

The theology of *The Good Place* highlights the absurdity of the religious system. Obsessing over the velvet ropes renders us incapable of obeying the one commandment that most of us agree to be the simplest explanation of the whole law: loving your neighbor as yourself. The law, as outlined by the "velvet ropes," will keep our neighbors hidden, out of sight, forgotten, cursed.[68]

This is mind-bending and convicting. And remarkable and freeing. It's not the people outside; it's the people inside who live under the power of the curse! Those in *The Good Place* may actually be in *The Bad Place*. The "religious guys" grip and regrip the law in a white-knuckled attempt to claim that God is against those on the outside.

---

67 *The Good Place*, Season 4, episode 3, "Tahani Al-Jamil," written by Aisha Muharrar, directed by Beth McCarthy-Miller, NBC.

68 Alison, *Undergoing God*, 202. Dr. Alison says it this way: "will hide that neighbor under the veil of being a 'cursed other.'"

But God isn't against *anyone*.

In light of all of this, in these last minutes before you go back into the different air pressure, to engage and reengage in the collective conversation with the religious person, I offer a caution: putting people over the text, mercy over sacrifice, and love over fear is a dangerous way to live. Be gentle as doves and wise as serpents.

It's often the religious people who are the most violent.

THE CONCLUSION WHERE I PRETEND TO BRING IT ALL TOGETHER

Ah yes, the conclusion, as if we can tie this up in a neat bow. But this isn't neat. It's messy. And the moment I get it organized, it un-organizes itself. Everything is in the process of change. Yes, fractal. It's astounding to consider how much has changed in my life over the last few years, but change, movement, and evolution are, of course, the way of the universe.

The explosion and forming stars,

the shifting and grinding tectonic plates,

the rolling and tossing ocean,

the blowing and moving wind,

the dying and birthing of people,

the dying and birthing of cells within your own body even as you read these words!

Nothing stays the same. Everything is in transition. It leaves me overwhelmed, but it also leaves me hopeful because if nothing ever stays the same, then my current problems may one day be influenced, affected, and changed. The possibility of change (yes, even an existential earthquake) introduces the possibility of redemption.

I am thankful for the earthquake of love I've experienced. I'm not thankful for the specific trauma that triggered the fault lines or the relationships that I've lost in the re-working out of my theology. But I am grateful for the chance to sift through the aftermath and build something with more structural integrity. Paradoxically, it's a structural integrity that leaves me a bit destabilized. While it is a rock of faith, it's less a rock that brings stability and more a rock upon which all my ideas broke upon, opening me up, exposing me, causing me to see my need for love.

By faith, I believe in love.

Our old religious systems talk a lot about faith. But, far too often, we're encouraged to have faith *in* Christ rather than a faith *of* Christ.[69] A faith *in* Christ puts the emphasis on what Christ did. It turns the death of Jesus into a transaction. Something we can stand apart from and worship. But a faith *of* Christ puts the emphasis on us following him. It's not something we can separate ourselves from. It's something that requires us to get involved.[70]

Faith is not a mental ascent, an objective affirmation of a belief, saying a creed, or an impersonal intellectual acceptance of God. Can one really know love intellectually? Probably not. God can only be loved and known in the *act* of love. God can only be experienced in relationship.

It seems the fundamental building block of the universe is relationship.[71] The energy in an atom, for example, is located neither in the proton, neutron, or electron. The energy can only be found in the interactive dance between the three particles. And when humanity ruptured that relationship on July 16, 1945, at a nuclear test site with the darkly poetic name of "Trinity," it

---

69 Ricahrd Rohr says this all better than me in places like: https://cac.org/faith-as-participation-2016-04-10/.

70 Matt 16:24 (NIV).

71 Delio, *The Unbearable Wholeness of Being*, 54–55. Catholic physicist Ilea Delio quotes Mark Herbert: "As we penetrate into matter, nature does not show us any isolated 'basic building blocks,' but rather appears as a complicated web of relations between the various parts of the whole."

created an atomic explosion; an earthquake, a wound. Our world has never been the same.

I can't help but think of my wife and me. Parents of three children. Like any parent's world, our world was comprised of an interactive dance between our children, and between the three-way relationship of father, mother, and children. When our daughter died, the three were ruptured. It was an existential atomic blast in our lives, an earthquake, a wound. Our world has never been the same.

And I can't help but think of the Trinity as an interactive dance between the three persons of that thing we have no other name for than God. When Jesus died, there was something akin to the splitting of an atom. I do not mean to say that the Father was at odds with the Son. Just that the rupturing of the Three released a kind of atomic outburst of pain and love, an earthquake, a wound. Our world has never been the same.

Nothing is stable. Things fold in on themselves again and again. The dimensions can't hold the weight; it's a kaleidoscopic giving way to that which is ever on the inside. Everything good *is* fractal.

Maybe one day, there will be no more mind-bending, soul-wrenching fractal and atomic wounds. Then again, maybe it's the wound that open us up to the reality of love. Either way, our only hope is love.

Sacrifice isn't strong enough.

Fear never lasts.

Rules eventually birth resentment.

The religious person's system has been exposed. It's not dependent upon God. It's dependent upon the behavior of the other.

Sigh …

Our only hope is love.

Merciful,

People-centered love.

By faith I believe that's our future.

May we live by the sound of that detonation now.

THE
BIBLIOGRAPHY
PART

Alison, James. *Undergoing God: Dispatches from the Scene of a Break-In*. London: Darton Longman and Todd, 2006.

Alison, James. *Faith Beyond Resentment: Fragments Catholic and Gay*. NY: Crossroads Publishing, 2001.

Have

Bell, Rob. *Everything is Spiritual*. NY: St. Martin's Essentials, 2020.

Berry, Steven E., and Michael Hardin. *Reading the Bible with René Girard: Conversations with Steven E. Berry*. Lancaster, PA: JDL Press, 2015.

Boersma, Hans; Daniels, T. Scott; Finger, Thomas N.; Weaver, J. Denny. *Atonement and Violence: A Theological Conversation*. Nashville, TN: Abingdon Press, 2006.

Boyd, Gregory A. *God of the Possible: A Biblical Introduction to the Open View of God*. Grand Rapids, MI: Baker Books, 2001.

Bruckner, James K. *Healthy Human Life: A Biblical Witness*. Eugene, OR: Cascade Books, 2012.

Brueggemann, Walter. *Prophetic Imagination: Revised Edition*. Lanham: Fortress Press, 2001.

Caputo, John. *The Weakness of God: A Theology of the Event*. Bloomington, IN: Indiana University Press, 2006.

Have Cone, James H. *The Cross and the Lynching Tree*. Maryknoll, NY: Orbis Books, 2019.

Delio, Ilia. *The Unbearable Wholeness of Being: God, Evolution, and the Power of Love*. Maryknoll, NY: Orbis Books, 2014.

Ellul, Jacques, and G. W. Bromiley. *The Subversion of Christianity*. Eugene, OR: Wipf & Stock Publishers, 2011.

Flood, Derek. *Disarming Scripture: Cherry-Picking Liberals, Violence-Loving Conservatives, and Why We All Need to Learn to Read the Bible Like Jesus Did*. San Francisco: Metanoia Books, 2014.

Fringer, Rob A. *Theology of Luck: Fate, Chaos, and Faith*. Kansas City, MO: Beacon Hill Press of Kansas City, 2015.

Girard, René. *Battling to the End: Conversations with Benoît Chantre (Studies in Violence, Mimesis & Culture)*. East Lansing: Michigan State University Press, 2010.

Girard René. *I See Satan Fall like Lightning.* New York: Orbis Books, 2011.

Hart, David Bentley. *That All Shall Be Saved: Heaven, Hell, and Universal Salvation.* New Haven: Yale University Press, 2019.

Jersak, Brad, and Michael Hardin. *Stricken by God?: Nonviolent Identification and the Victory of Christ.* Grand Rapids, MI: William B. Eerdmans, 2007.

Jersak, Brad. *Her Gates Will Never Be Shut: Hell, Hope, and the New Jerusalem.* Eugene, OR: Wipf & Stock Publishers, 2010.

Jersak, Brad. *A More Christlike God: A More Beautiful Gospel.* Place of publication not identified: PLAIN TRUTH MINISTRIES, 2016.

Karris, Mark Gregory. *Religious Refugees: (De)constructing Toward Spiritual and Emotional Health.* Orange: Quoir, 2020.

Keller, Catherine. *The Face of the Deep: A Theology of Becoming.* NY: Routledge, 2003.

Oord, Thomas J. *Uncontrolling Love: An Open and Relational Account of Providence.* Downers Grove, IL: InterVarsity Press, 2015.

Have

Oord, Thomas J. *God Can't: How to Believe in God and Love after Tragedy, Abuse, and Other Evils.* SacraSage Press, 2019.

Read
Rohr, Richard. *Everything Belongs: The Gift of Contemplative Prayer.* New York: The Crossroad Publishing Company, 2014.

Rollins, Peter. *The Idolatry of God.* New York: Howard Books, 2012.

Have
Spufford, Francis. *Unapologetic: Why, Despite Everything, Christianity Can Still Make Surprising Emotional Sense.* New York: HarperOne, 2014.

Read
Taylor, Barbara Brown. *Leaving Church: A Memoir of Faith.* Norwich: Canterbury Press Norwich, 2011.

Have
Walton, John H. *The Lost World of Adam and Eve: Genesis 2–3 and the Human Origins Debate.* Downers Grove, IL: IVP Academic, 2015.

Wiesel, Ellie. *Night:* New York: Hill & Wang, 1960.

Wink, Walter. *Homosexuality and Christian Faith: Questions of Conscience for the Churches.* Minneapolis, MN: Fortress Press, 1999.

Have
Wink, Walter. *The Powers That Be: Theology for a New Millennium.* New York: Doubleday, 1999.

Zahnd, Brian. *Beauty Will Save the World: Rediscovering the Allure & Mystery of Christianity*. Lake Mary, FL: Charisma House, 2012.

Have
Zahnd, Brian. *Sinners in the Hands of a Loving God: The Scandalous Truth of the Very Good News*. CO Springs, CO: WaterBrook, 2017.

ABOUT THE AUTHOR

Jonathan Foster is the award-winning author of the following books …

- *Where Was God on the Worst Day of My Life*

- *Death, Hope, and the Laughter of God: An Unlikely Title About the Unlikely Path Where God Finds Us*

- *Questions about Sexuality that Got Me Uninvited from My Denomination*

- *The Hope and Melvin of Humanity and Other Surprising Short Stories*

There was something of a breakthrough with *The Reconstructionist* as it was his first book with less than ten words in the title.

The faith community evolving at missiofaith.life is where he spends a lot of his time, and he's incredibly proud of what's happening at LQVE.org. When he's not with his family, he's reading Rene Girard or Open and Relational Theology. Or both. To find out more about what he's up to, make sure to sign up for the e-newsletter at his website, and when you do, you'll receive some more of his writing. (A classic win-win). You can make all that happen at jonathanfosteronline.com.

For more information about Jonathan J. Foster
or to contact him for speaking engagements,
please visit *www.JonathanFosterOnline.com*

Many voices. One message.

Quoir is a boutique publisher
with a singular message: *Christ is all.*
Venture beyond your boundaries to discover Christ
in ways you never thought possible.

For more information, please visit
www.quoir.com

CPSIA information can be obtained
at www.ICGtesting.com
Printed in the USA
BVHW040821181221
624348BV00005B/607